Longitude West of Greenwich

Longitude East of Greenwich

From Classroom Atlas: 1994 Edition
© 1994 by Rand McNally, R.L. 94-S-11

Sinusoidal Projection
SCALE 1:36,313,000 1 Inch = 565 Statute Miles

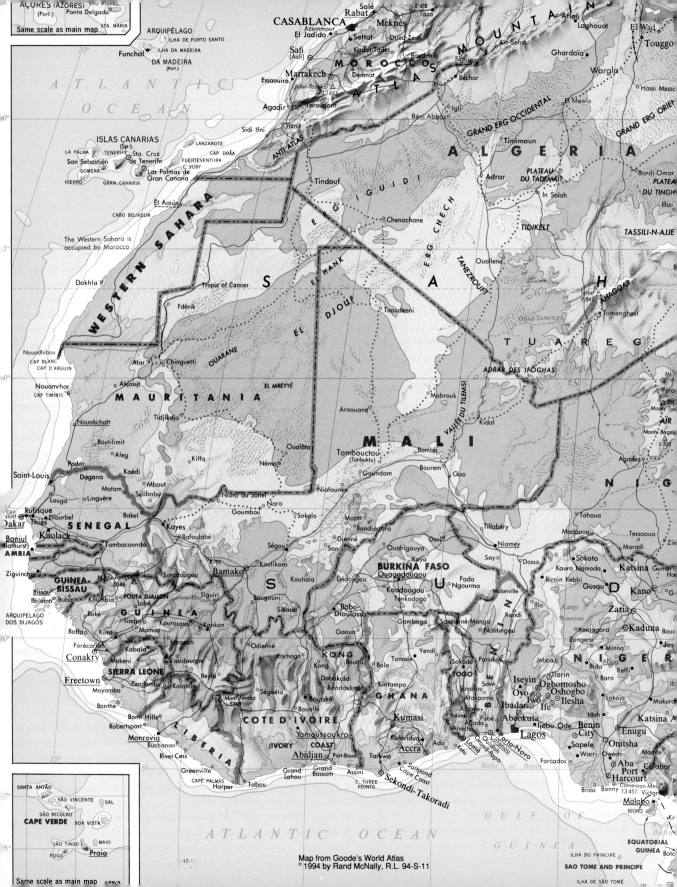

Map from Goode's World Atlas
© 1994 by Rand McNally, R.L. 94-S-11

Enchantment of the World

THE GAMBIA

By Robert Zimmermann

Consultant for The Gambia: Judith Carney, Ph.D., Department of
Geography, University of California, Los Angeles

Consultant for Reading: Robert L. Hillerich, Ph.D., Professor Emeritus,
Bowling Green State University; Consultant, Pinellas County Schools, Florida

CHILDRENS PRESS®

CHICAGO

A tailor making clothes in his on-the-street shop

Project Editor: Mary Reidy
Design: Margrit Fiddle

Library of Congress Cataloging-in-Publication Data

Zimmermann, Robert (Robert B.)
    The Gambia / by Robert Zimmermann.
        p.   cm. – (Enchantment of the world)
    Includes index.
    Summary: Discusses the geography, history, government, people, and culture of The Gambia.
    ISBN 0-516-02625-9
    1. Gambia–Juvenile literature. [1. Gambia.]
I. Title. II. Series.
DT509.22.Z56 1994   94-7008
966.51–dc20   CIP
                                            AC

Picture Acknowledgments
Bettmann: 17 (bottom left)
The Bettmann Archive: 29, 45
© **Dave G. Houser:** 6 (bottom), 20, 22, 24, 34, 36 (right), 76, 79, 87 (left), 93 (right), 109

© **Wolfgang Kaehler:** Cover, 6 (top), 8, 12, 18 (right), 61, 66, 67 (left), 68, 69, 74, 75 (left), 85, 87 (right), 89, 91 (left). 107 (2 photos), 108, 110 (bottom right)
North Wind Picture Archives: 31, 32, 37, 47
Photri: 10, 48, 88, 99
Premaphotos Wildlife: © **K.G. Preston-Mafham,** 9, 14 (right), 19 (top right), 73
© **Carl Purcell:** 21
Reuters/Bettmann: 57, 60
Stock Montage: 27, 30
Tony Stone Images: © **Hilarie Kavanagh,** 83
SuperStock International, Inc.: © **Hubertus Kanus,** 51, 64, 93 (left)
UN Photo: © **M. Grant,** (1884292, Doc 48-GA), 59
UPI/Bettmann Newsphotos: 36 (left), 55
Valan: © **C. Osborne,** 4, 5, 15, 62, 63, 64 (inset), 66 (inset), 67 (right), 70 (2 photos), 72 (2 photos), 75 (right), 80, 81, 90, 91 (right), 96, 101, 102, 104, 105, 110 (top and bottom left), 111, 112; © **Tom W. Parkin,** 14 (left); © **Arthur Christiansen,** 17 (top left), 19 (bottom left); © **Jeff Foott,** 17 (top right); © **Val & Alan Wilkinson,** 17 (center left); © **James D. Markou,** 17 (center right); © **Stephen J. Krasemann,** 17 (bottom right); © **B. Lyon,** 18 (left), 19 (top left and bottom right)
Len W. Meents: Maps on 65, 75, 77
Courtesy Flag Research Center, Winchester, Massachusetts 01890: Flag on back cover
Cover: Women and children gather for an Independence celebration in Jambur village

A wood carver at work

TABLE OF CONTENTS

Above: Egrets along the Gambia River
Below: The port of Banjul

Chapter 1

BETWEEN OCEAN

AND DESERT

In West Africa, too small to be noticed at first glance, is the tiny country of The Gambia. A closer look reveals that this country consists of the banks along a single river, the Gambia River. The country is called *The* Gambia to distinguish it from the Gambia River. This river slices straight into the continent where the bulge of West Africa is greatest. Almost surrounding this little nation is the much bigger country of Senegal. The Gambia's size and shape have amused some people. One reporter called it "the Gambian hot dog in the Senegalese roll."

But there is nothing funny about The Gambia. It continues to exist as an independent country. This is something everyone said was impossible thirty years ago. It is a poor country but it has used the little money available carefully. Starvation and misery are not to be found. The Gambia stands out as one of the most peaceful and one of the most democratic nations in Africa.

A boatload of tourists in the mangrove swamps at the estuary of the Gambia River

The Gambia has an area of 4,361 square miles (11,295 square kilometers), a bit smaller than the state of Connecticut. Small as the country is, The Gambia is a meeting place for the two most important features of West Africa. On one side lies the mighty Atlantic Ocean. On the other lies the edge of the Sahara, the largest desert in the world.

LANDSCAPE

There are three physical regions in The Gambia: the coast, the flat lowlands lying along the river, and the slightly higher and drier uplands. The most important feature of The Gambia's coast is the mouth of the Gambia River, a wide, deep, flooded river valley. This type of river mouth is called an *estuary*. Estuaries are different from rivers; they have tides because of the influence of the sea.

Palm trees grow inland from the Atlantic Ocean.

Salt water from the Atlantic Ocean flows 56 miles (90 kilometers) upriver. For another 99 miles (159 kilometers) the river is mixed salt and freshwater. Upstream the river is freshwater. Agriculture in this area has adapted to these differences.

The coastal area is made up of sands and clays that the ocean has been building up slowly for thousands of years. Miles of clean sandy beaches face the Atlantic Ocean. The Atlantic sometimes crashes against the coast with waves so large and violent that swimming and launching boats are hazardous. At other times the Atlantic is still and gentle, perfect for swimming. Inland are groves of palm trees and lagoons.

Most of the country lies parallel to the river. On either side of this waterway are floodplains, land that is partially submerged by the river in the wet season. Most of The Gambia's food production and animal life are concentrated here. Because the river is salty downstream, not much besides mangroves grows in the salty plains of this part of the country. In the middle stretches of the river,

Harvesting rice

where salt water is present only in the dry season, rice is grown following the rains. At the eastern end where fresh river water is always present, rice is grown in both the rainy and the dry seasons.

The rest of the country, away from the floodplains, consists of the sandstone uplands, sandy soils that depend on rainfall, rather than river tides, for water. Although not high in elevation, these areas are called uplands because they are above river flooding. The Gambia is a low, flat country where maximum altitude is only 239 feet (73 meters). These sandstone hills and rolling plateaus are much drier than the floodplains. In the dry season they seem like deserts because the trees and grasses shrivel and turn yellow, but in the five-month wet season from June to October they are green and covered with vegetation. The uplands are where most of the people live and where most of the roads lie. Here are grown the groundnuts (peanuts) that are The Gambia's main source of income.

CLIMATE

The Gambia's climate is a direct result of its location between the Atlantic and the Sahara. There are two distinct seasons, defined by the absence or presence of rain. The temperature is very hot during much of the dry season and less hot but more humid during the rains. From June through October the winds come off the ocean bringing rain. November to May is the dry season, when the winds shift directions and blow out of the Sahara.

This area in Africa bordering the Sahara in called the *Sahel*, "shore" in Arabic. Here the amount of rainfall is not always the main problem for agricultural survival. More important is the arrival of the wet season and the distribution of the rain that falls. This can vary greatly from one year to another.

The influence of the Atlantic Ocean can be seen in different weather patterns, even in this tiny country. The interior averages nearly 100 degrees Fahrenheit (37.7 degrees Celsius) annually but is hotter in the dry season and more muggy during the rains. But along the coast cool breezes blow off the ocean and sometimes at night during the months of December and January, the temperature can drop to 60 degrees Fahrenheit (15.5 degrees Celsius), cool enough to require blankets and sweaters.

Depending on global climatic cycles, the Sahara expands or shrinks by as much as 87 miles (140 kilometers) a year. During the 1960s through the mid-1980s the Sahara expanded to the south, bringing drought conditions to The Gambia. By the 1990s wetter conditions returned and the Sahara moved 68 miles (109 kilometers) northward.

An unwelcome participant in the dry season is the wind known as the *harmattan* that blows out of the Sahara. Essentially, this wind carries fine sand with it, which sometimes creates a dust

The air is filled with dust when the harmattan is blowing.

blizzard that may make it impossible to see much more than a few feet ahead. Trees and buildings become ghostly objects. When the harmattan is particularly fierce, the sun looks like a weak lightbulb. Fortunately the harmattan occurs in the driest months when there is little farming, so people are able to go indoors during the days when conditions are serious.

The shift from the dry to the wet season occurs with the arrival of clouds that grow in height to become thunderheads by late May. The storms begin in late afternoon. Huge violet-gray clouds like fists appear overhead. As the wind picks up, large drops of water begin to fall. Rainwater suddenly pounds the thirsty earth in massive waves. Everything turns dark. There is the roar of nearby thunder and the sky glows from bright lightning. The next day the dust has vanished, the sun shines, and within days the soaked earth gives birth to tiny blades of bright green grass. The wet season has begun, planting for food begins, and the cycle of life experiences an awakening.

VEGETATION

The term used to describe The Gambia's grassland vegetation overall is *savanna*. Scattered trees grow out of the tall grass and the vegetation changes dramatically with the seasons. In the wet season everything is green. In the dry season everything withers and dies except the trees, although most of them lose their leaves. Typical trees that rise out of the grass are the towering *kapok*, or silk cotton, with its fluffy white flowers that look like feathers and are used to stuff mattresses. Along the coast are various types of palm trees, which give fruit, oil, and wine.

The baobab or upside-down tree looks like it was pulled from the earth and placed wrong side up. The baobab is an important feature of the landscape. It grows to be seventy feet (twenty-one meters) tall. But even more unique is its barrellike trunk, which can have a circumference of thirty feet (nine meters). The baobab is an extremely useful tree. Its flowers are sweet smelling and the leaves can be eaten or used to make medicine. The large yellow fruit can be made into a thirst-quenching beverage or into medicine for illness related to poor blood circulation. Because the fruit is the favorite of monkeys, the Africans call it the monkey bread tree. The hollows of its huge trunk enable villages to store water during periods of drought. In certain places the hollow trunk is used as the burial place of *griots* (the "t" is not pronounced), storytellers or the country's oral historians. According to custom the bodies of griots cannot be placed next to the bodies of other people.

The baobab bark is made into paper, rope, and cloth. The seeds are used to make fertilizer and soap. When the tree dies, the wood is used for firewood. The baobab's importance is reflected

Left: Inside the seed pods of the kapok tree are the fluffy white flowers used to stuff mattresses. Right: The baobab tree

in its repeated appearance in popular folk tales and myths. It is often considered to have magical properties.

What the baobab is to the uplands, the mangrove tree is to the floodplains beside the ocean and the salty parts of the river. It grows in the salty tidal mudflats at the edge of the water. Salt water kills most plants, but the mangrove will not grow unless salt water is present. This tropical evergreen, whose roots reach up above the water a long way from the trunk, can be found 80 miles (129 kilometers) up the Gambia River. A total of more than 2,000 miles (3,219 kilometers) of The Gambia's coastline and inland waterways are lined by mangrove forests.

The mangrove has many trunks, all thin enough to look like branches going in all directions. The bare roots stick out of the watery mud like spider legs. The mangrove can grow to eighty feet (twenty-four meters) in height. The mangrove captures mud

The roots of the mangroves hold soil and keep it from washing away.

and sand among its roots until enough has gathered to create dry land. In doing so, the mangrove's roots function like giant staples that keep the coastal land and the sandy ground farther back from washing away. When the leaves and wood fall into the mud, the mud is slowly thickened and becomes excellent farming land.

Fishers in canoes visit the mangroves to catch shellfish like shrimp, oysters, and crabs. Hunters also go to the mangroves to find duck and other wildfowl.

The mangrove also helps to filter waste found in the water. Its wood is excellent for firewood, for carving, and for home building. Such usefulness has led to massive destruction of mangrove forests in several parts of the world, but not yet in The Gambia.

ANIMAL LIFE

The Sahara was once an area of lush vegetation with plentiful water supplies. It was crowded with large animals such as the elephant, buffalo, giraffe, lion, and wildebeest. That lasted until about seven thousand years ago. By five thousand years ago the world's climate had changed, and the animals migrated to eastern Africa, where they are now. While The Gambia is not actually in the Sahara, its nearness to it has meant that its animal population has been affected by what happened there. Today there are almost no large animals in The Gambia. The Gambia's fauna, crocodiles and hippopotamuses, are mostly found along the river's banks.

Away from the river and its creeks live warthogs, baboons, and the duiker and oribi (both dwarf antelopes). Birds include hawks, eagles of various types, buzzards, crows, pintailed weavers, wydah birds, and ospreys. There are snakes such as the mamba and python; the armor-plated giant pangolin, a mammal with horny scales; scorpions; spiders; and the aardvark and its food, termites.

Animal life exists in the greatest quantity and variety on the uninhabited islands of the river and the creeks. Typically there are tall trees in the middle of an island with mangrove forests occupying the edges. In this dense plant growth live olive baboons, green-coated vervet monkeys with their white "bibs," patas monkeys with red "jackets," and the rare colobus monkey. Swimming in the nearby water are four-foot (one-meter) long monitor lizards and pythons. Around islands in freshwater areas upriver are crocodiles, reaching up to 15 feet (4.5 meters) in length, and a few hippopotamuses.

Some creatures
found living in
The Gambia are,
clockwise from
top left,
vervet monkeys,
giant pangolins,
black and white colobus
monkeys, warthogs,
monitor lizards,
and blue duikers.

Left: The waterbuck is a river animal.
Above: A huge termite hill

Other river animals are the boar, the waterbuck, the hoopoe bird, the glossy ibis, the water chevrotain (a rabbit-size deer), francolins (a type of partridge), and waterbirds such as waders and rails. All the elephants mentioned by explorers in the eighteenth century are gone. All that remains as a remembrance is the name of Elephant Island. Today, the largest animals that live here are monkeys.

As in all tropical countries, insects abound. The termites build towerlike structures in the countryside, often twice the height of a human being. These are the highrise homes of millions of these insects.

Many winged visitors spend a few days or weeks in the Gambia before continuing their long-distance travels. These birds spend summers in Europe to the north and the winters in central Africa. Their flyway or travel route skirts around the inhospitable

Interesting birds in The Gambia are the blue-cheeked bee eater (top left), the Barbary shrike (top right), the Abyssinian roller (bottom left), and the spur-winged plover (left).

Sahara by following the Atlantic coast south. Some birds enjoy The Gambia so much they remain there all winter. More than four hundred species can be seen, including such rarely observed birds as bar-tailed godwits, long-tailed shags, buff-backed herons, spur-winged plovers, blue-cheeked bee-eaters, Abyssinian rollers, and Barbary shrikes. Such a concentration of exotic birds brings other "winged" visitors, the European bird-watchers who flock to The Gambia during the months of November to April with binoculars in one hand and cameras in the other.

Apes in Abuko Native Reserve are studied by scientists.

The government has made efforts to protect The Gambia's wildlife. In 1977 President Sir D. K. Jawara signed the Banjul Declaration urging Gambians and visitors to respect the country's flora and fauna. He also pledged that the government would attempt to preserve as much as possible. There are several nature reserves, one on the coast and five inland. Some, like the chimpanzee rehabilitation project on Baboon Island, are closed to visitors. However, the Abuko Nature Reserve south of Banjul is open. It preserves a stretch of primary Gambian rain forest and is populated by crocodiles, birds, monkeys, squirrels, and antelopes. It is also the only successful ape rehabilitation center in the world.

Baboons live on Baboon Island National Park.

Here chimpanzees, baboons, and gorillas born in captivity in zoos or circuses of Europe and America are taught to survive in nature. After their training they are released on Baboon Island National Park, halfway up the Gambia River.

The waters off the bulge of West Africa where The Gambia is located are well known to sport and commercial fishers all over the world as a rich fishing area. The winds that blow out of the Sahara push the surface of the ocean away from the land, allowing colder water to come up from below. A cold water current runs off the coast, and the colder water provides nutrients that nourish a large supply of tiny marine life. This attracts and supports a great variety of fish. Game fish such as marlin, barracuda, sailfish, bonito, swordfish, shark, huge ocean sunfish, and capitaine are some that swim in these waters.

THE RIVER

The Gambia River is one of West Africa's major physical features. It is 1,100 miles (1,770 kilometers) long. Its drainage

Crocodiles and water lilies along the banks of the Gambia River

begins in the highlands of the country of Guinea, to the southeast. From there it flows through the dry savannas of southeastern Senegal. Eight hundred miles (1,287 kilometers) from its source the river enters The Gambia, where it winds back and forth. From the country's eastern border to the town of Georgetown about 162 miles (261 kilometers) upriver, the river flows between raised banks covered with thick foliage. Monkeys and baboons jump about in the trees and bark as boats go by. Downriver from Georgetown the river widens and often divides, forming numerous mid-river islands.

Farther downstream mudflats and mangrove swamps line the banks. A number of creeks, called *bolons* or *bolongs*, enter from both sides. Sand that was eroded as the river passed through the sandstone uplands collects at certain places on the river's bottom. These become sandbanks that are a danger to navigation.

The estuary, near the mouth, is not impressive from the ground.

But on a map or from the air one can see how the river spreads dramatically at its last bend. There are four to five miles (six to eight kilometers) of water between the banks. After narrowing a bit near Dog Island, the estuary widens to as much as nine miles (fourteen kilometers). This was one of the sheltered, deep harbors that the early European explorers and traders needed so badly when they sailed down the bulge of West Africa. Nevertheless, there are hazardous sandbars here too that are constantly moving under the water, but they are not big enough to block shipping. Past Banjul, the country's main city and capital, the river flows into the Atlantic Ocean. From an airplane the mud-colored waters of the river can be seen flowing out into the blue Atlantic before they become mixed with ocean water by wind and currents.

POPULATION

The population of the country was approximately 750,000 in 1987. The population increases about 3.49 percent each year. Although one out of five Gambian children dies before reaching age five, the majority of the population is under the age of twenty. Only a small percentage is elderly. The population increase is the result of major improvements in health care and immunization programs during the last twenty years of the twentieth century.

The Gambia's population is divided into five major ethnic groups: the Mandinka (the "roots" of Alex Haley's ancestors), Wolof, Fulani, Serrahuli, and Jola. Also found are people from neighboring countries, Lebanese traders, and a small group of European advisers, businessmen, and diplomats.

The Senegambian Stone Circles, which are about six feet (two meters) high, are situated on the dry uplands in the middle of the country.

Chapter 2

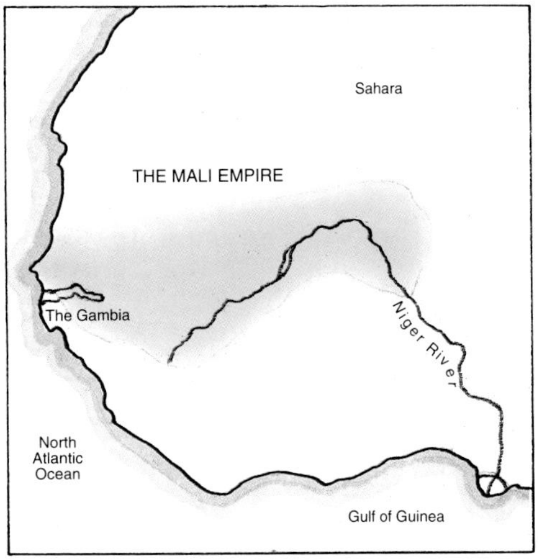

SAHELIAN EMPIRES AND EUROPEAN TRADERS

The map shows the Mali Empire, with labels for Sahara, THE MALI EMPIRE, The Gambia, North Atlantic Ocean, Niger River, and Gulf of Guinea.

ROOTS

The Gambia's historical roots are not easy for historians to trace. Before the Europeans arrived there was no written language. Only three historical sources exist, and they are incomplete or difficult to understand. The first is the Senegambian Stone Circles, ancient mysterious circles of stone that sit on the dry uplands in the middle of the country. (Senegambia is the term used to describe the area now occupied by Senegal and The Gambia.) Another source is the griots, the chanting oral historians or storytellers, who are trained in memory retention. They recount legends and events affecting their communities that have been passed down for hundreds of years through many generations. However, much of this knowledge was lost because of the vast number of Gambians who were uprooted by the slave trade. Lastly there exist oral and written records left by Arab traders from North Africa who visited the area.

The first humans to populate Senegambia were nomads who were attracted to the abundant animal life and vegetation that then existed near the river. By three thousand years ago people were living in permanent settlements. They cultivated rice, millet, and sorghum (cereal grasses), and fermented wine from the local palm trees. These Gambian farmers already had a sophisticated knowledge of their environment. They advanced rapidly into the Iron Age once the technology was introduced from East Africa. This process was made easier by the abundance of iron deposits along the banks of the Gambia River. Some scholars think these iron-smelting Gambians erected the stone circles.

The stone circles consist of ten to twenty stumps of reddish stone that vary in size and have flat or concave tops. They are found in Senegambia and Mali, a country that is mainly east and northeast of The Gambia, and no one knows why they were built. The circles were constructed between the eighth and the twelfth centuries A.D. They have been referred to as one of Africa's greatest riddles. In The Gambia there are about forty of these sites on the uplands north of the river. There may have been streams there at the time. The sites bear witness to the existence of a sophisticated, civilized culture. In the center of some of the circles, skeletons and pottery, along with tools, weapons, and ornaments made of iron, copper, brass, and gold, have been discovered. It is thought that these were burial sites of chiefs.

THE SAHELIAN EMPIRES

Beginning about the third century A.D. three empires developed along the great bend of the Niger River in an area centered on the inland Niger Delta in present-day Mali. This area, called the

A drawing of buildings in the kingdom of Mali

Sahelian zone, is on the southern fringe of the Sahara. Great wealth was attained by taxing and providing services for the trade in gold, ivory, kola nuts, and salt between North Africa and the southern coast of West Africa. Splendid cities, great universities, and mighty armies called this area home during the time of Europe's Middle Ages.

Though on the western edge of these savanna Sahelian Empires, Senegambia was profoundly influenced by them. The first of the influential empires was that of Ghana (which bears no geographic relationship to the country of the same name, but covered the system of ancient trade routes linking the present-day countries of Mauritania and Mali). It existed roughly from the fifth through the twelfth centuries A.D., the same period when the stone circles were built. The interest its rulers took in Senegambia was probably owing to the iron deposits along the Gambia River. In the eleventh century A.D. North African warriors were attracted by Ghana's gold reserves. The North Africans conquered the people and began the process of conversion to their religion, Islam. However, the efforts of the invaders to convert the people of Senegambia were not totally successful. Many groups resisted. This was especially true of the people south of the Gambia River.

The next influential empire was that of Mali, which lasted from the thirteenth to the fifteenth centuries A.D., just prior to

European arrival. This empire was created by the Bambara speakers (a language close to Mandinka or Mandingo). They dominated Senegambia throughout this period and forced such ethnic groups as the Wolof, Serer, and Tukolor to convert to Islam. Trade between Senegambia and the interior continued.

When the empire of Mali fell in the fifteenth century, a period of political turmoil as well as economic breakdown followed. Different groups from the north and east settled in Senegambia. They brought their cultures and created an astonishing mixture of people that still exists today. For example, the sophisticated Mandinkas invaded Senegambia and overpowered groups that had been there for centuries. Islamic *jihads*, or holy wars, brought into Gambia many Fulani people, who spread the Muslim religion.

EXPLORATION OF WEST AFRICA

The first Europeans to attempt to explore West Africa were from the Mediterranean area. These nations were well versed in sailing and trade. Voyages took place between 2000 B.C. and A.D. 100. Around 600 B.C. a group of Phoenicians sailed around the bulge and may have explored the mouth of the Gambia River. One hundred years later the Carthaginians sailed the West African coast and also stopped at a river mouth, possibly the Gambia's. Records from classical Greece note that a Greek ship captain returned from West Africa around 300 B.C. with descriptions of a river full of crocodiles and hippopotamuses. With the disintegration of the Roman Empire, the Mediterranean world turned inward and sub-Saharan Africa was forgotten by Europeans for a thousand years.

*Prince Henry the Navigator
of Portugal*

THE PORTUGUESE

By the fifteenth century A.D. Europe was emerging politically
and becoming economically more powerful. Spain and Portugal
took advantage of their successful expulsion of the Muslim
kingdoms occupying the Iberian Peninsula to invade North Africa.
Then they turned their attention to the world trade routes
controlled by the Arabs and the northern Italians.

Portugal, located on the Atlantic Ocean and the first of the
Iberian countries to expel the Muslims, led the way. Under the
leadership of Prince Henry the Navigator, the Portuguese set up a
special support center with the best maps, charts, and sailors of
Europe. Their goal was to gain control of the southern West

Workers in the salt trade

African coast. Then they could divert the gold and salt trade across the Sudan and Sahara to a sea route around the bulge of West Africa ending in Portugal. They eventually succeeded.

To achieve their goal the Portuguese had to leave the part of the world that they knew. The edge of that world was Cape Bojador on the African coast (in present-day Western Sahara) south of the Canary Islands. Information about what lay beyond was either incomplete or considered highly untrustworthy. Though he sent out the best mariners he could hire, Prince Henry's expeditions failed for many years.

Cape Bojador was finally left behind in 1432. After that the Portuguese gradually advanced down the coast. In 1444 they reached the mouth of the Senegal River and saw the first green vegetation after 600 miles (966 kilometers) of desert coastline. Here there were difficult sailing conditions. When trade winds blew, the result was huge Atlantic waves that could smash small boats trying to land.

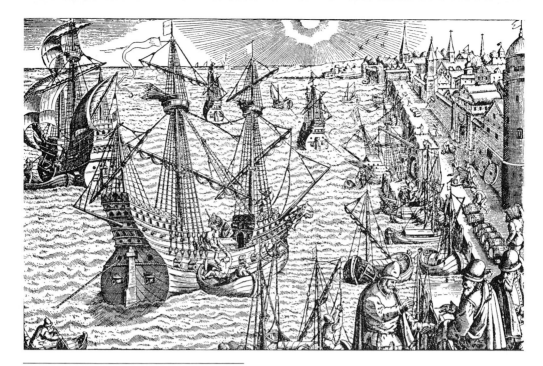

Small wooden ships fill the busy harbor of Lisbon, Portugal, in the fifteenth century.

But north and south of Dakar (the present-day capital of Senegal) the estuaries begin along the coast. From Senegal south to The Gambia the first estuaries the Portuguese found were those of the Senegal, the Saloum, the Gambia, and the Casamance rivers. The Senegal and the Saloum were blocked by sandbars, a typical problem of West African river mouths.

The Gambia's estuary was, therefore, a welcome sight when the Portuguese sailed in for the first time in 1445. Here, finally, was a place of quiet, deep water, sheltered from the churning Atlantic. And if its width was any indication, it held out the promise of leading deep into Africa, where wealth lay waiting. Even after the Europeans abandoned the slave trade in this area, the Gambia River remained important. Its attraction as a safe haven for ships traveling the coast led to many years of rivalry between European powers who wanted to establish protective forts near the mouth. The country that exists today carries the river's name, not vice versa.

Senegambian men and women were captured to be used as slave labor.

The Portuguese were met with the open and welcoming curiosity of a people who had not seen foreigners arrive by ship. But as traffic in slavery accompanied the earliest Portuguese voyages, the curiosity of local peoples soon turned to conflict with the Europeans. The Portuguese set the stage for the enslavement of African people, who provided labor for the plantations of the New World–the Caribbean, the southern United States, and Latin America. The extent of the enslavement of Senegambians was so vast that in South Carolina today 20 percent of the African-American population are descended from the people of this area. Eventually a small settlement was built to trade in goods as well as human beings. Many Portuguese died of tropical diseases. The survivors intermarried with local ethnic groups, and their hardier offspring dominated the emergent Portuguese-West African trading network.

The desire to control world trade routes drove the Portuguese on down the coast of Africa. In 1487-1488 the Portuguese rounded the southernmost point of the continent and sailed into the Indian Ocean. By 1500 the Portuguese had sailed westward from the West African coast to Brazil in South America. Their traffic in African slaves linked the peoples of the Americas, Africa, and Europe in new ways. One important outcome was the transfer of food crops between Brazil and West Africa. From the native Americans in Brazil the Portuguese brought pineapples, cashews, manioc, tobacco, and peanuts, the main export crop for The Gambia today. Crops domesticated in Africa—oil palms, yams, sorghum, millet, and rice—were sent to Brazil and the Caribbean.

STRUGGLE FOR THE RIVER

Economic and political changes in Europe during the second half of the sixteenth century weakened Spain and Portugal as world powers. They were replaced by France, the Netherlands, and England. The resulting rivalries among these three for control of world trade had an impact on many parts of the non-European world, including The Gambia.

The typical pattern followed by the Europeans was to set up a temporary trading station or a permanent, fortified trading post, preferably on an island for improved defense. These were built on land that was rented, bought, or simply given by a local king. The posts were manned by small garrisons. Slave trade continued from the mid-fifteenth century, for nearly four hundred years.

In 1651 traders from the small Baltic country of Courland (part of present-day Latvia) arrived looking for slaves to send to their Caribbean colony of Tobago. They built a fort on an island

Remains of the fort on James Island

strategically located where the estuary narrows slightly. It later became known as James Island. No sooner had the fort been built than English traders ejected the Courlanders. The year was 1661. The English would be periodically forced out of James Island by the Dutch, the French, and pirates, but prevailed because of their economic strength. The fort remained important for organizing the slave trade in The Gambia, and the island garrison remained with its sickly European staff of sailors and traders and its stockade of large numbers of African slaves.

Because poor nutrition and overwork resulted in high mortality rates, the growing demand for slaves on European plantations in the New World continued. The average life span for a slave on a sugar plantation was seven years. The slave trade also had a pronounced effect on Gambian society. Different ethnic groups went to war against each other. Warfare consisted of attacking villages, which were burned to the ground if they did not surrender. The men were sold as slaves and the women emerged as the principal farmers for food production. War stopped in the rainy season when mobility declined because of muddy conditions. Out of these struggles, village units developed into clans and finally into kingdoms. These were based principally on the wealth of village agriculture and the slave trade.

In the second half of the seventeenth century the French became the main competitors of the English in West Africa. They captured Dutch forts along the coast of Senegal and, by treaty with a local king, laid claim to the entire north bank of the Gambia River. In 1681 the French Senegal Company built a trading post opposite James Island. They called it Albreda. French ships stopped and seized English ships trading along the coast. The English company struck back. In the following decades Albreda was destroyed and rebuilt over and over.

While European-Gambian relations in Bathurst and the surrounding areas under the Gambian chief had begun as basically friendly, they had cooled considerably after the French arrived in the 1680s. The French continued to occupy Albreda, even though they had to sail past Bathurst on the opposite side of the river's mouth to get there. But in 1857, with trade guarantees, the French ceded Albreda to the British. By this time the French were firmly in control of a large territory that encircled the Gambia River. This was the French colony of Senegal, north, east, and south of The Gambia. Its capital, Dakar, became the administrative center for all French colonies in West Africa. It was a lot bigger and wealthier than the Colony of The Gambia.

During the American War of Independence, from 1775 to 1783,

The author Alex Haley with his book Roots *(left)
and people of Juffure today (above)*

British officers at the James Island fort seized American slave
ships trading at Albreda. But the French, allies of the Americans,
damaged the fort on St. James to such an extent that it was
abandoned for good. Today James Island has only a few vine-
covered walls and rust-covered cannons sitting in the tropical sun
and rain.

At the same time Africans, including Gambians, were resisting
the slave trade. By 1800 nearly twelve million Africans had been
seized for the slave trade. The Gambia remained important in the
slave trade until that trade was abolished. The Gambia River was
full of slave ships flying the flags of Britain, France, the United
States, Portugal, Spain, Denmark, and Prussia. During the
eighteenth century more than three thousand slaves were shipped
from Senegambia each year.

An extremely popular book and television series focused

A slave ship being pursued by a British patrol ship

attention on what happened along the Gambia River. In 1976 an African-American by the name of Alex Haley published a book entitled *Roots*. It was his attempt to find out who his ancestors were. Haley traced them back to a Mandinka-speaking young man who lived in the Gambian village of Juffure on the river's north bank, near Albreda, before he was enslaved and sent to the United States. This book was a huge success and was followed by a television version, which also was well received. As a result Juffure is today a main attraction to African-American visitors to The Gambia.

Toward the beginning of the nineteenth century the British achieved control over many countries and most of the oceans, and therefore trade routes, of the world. This meant that non-British ships could no longer enter the Gambia River at will. When the British abolished slavery in 1807, their navy was instructed to patrol the west coast of Africa, capture slave ships, and return slaves to Africa. Recaptured slaves, often from unknown regions, were established in British-controlled areas, at Freetown in present-day Sierra Leone south of The Gambia and on St. Mary's

Island, an island at the beginning of the Gambia River estuary. Today the Christian descendants of these people in The Gambia are known as Aku. The abolition of slavery provided an excuse for the British government to establish an area adjoining the mouth of the Gambia River as the official Colony of The Gambia. The days when private companies ruled the area came to an end.

With abolition in the nineteenth century, the trade in slaves was being replaced with trade in forest and animal products: wax from beehives located in the forests, ivory from the elephants, and hides from Fulani cattle. In addition, there was a new product, the peanut, which had been introduced from Brazil. Traders were anxious to load their ships with peanuts, hides, and wax brought down the river to Banjul from the interior uplands.

THE TOWN OF THE FREE

In 1816 the British secretary of state, Lord Bathurst, ordered construction of a new fort at the mouth of the Gambia River. St. Mary's Island was selected as the site. This was possible thanks to support from the king of Kombo, who asked in exchange that the British protect his kingdom from slavers and provide him with 103 bars of iron per year, which could be melted for agricultural tools and weapons. This fort became the town of Banjul.

A fort was built with barracks for the soldiers and a battery of six 24-pound cannons. It was named, of course, after Lord Bathurst. Civilian settlers were desired, too, so small plots of free land were offered to freed slaves for farming in the province. British troops provided a stable political setting for trade. Traders flocked to the colony from both the Gambia and the Senegal rivers. They were soon joined by African (particularly Wolof) traders from Senegalese ports to the north. By 1819 there were seven hundred civilians, of which only thirty were Europeans. During the dry season trading period (November to May) as many as forty trading ships might drop anchor nearby. By 1825 the number of civilians had increased to fourteen hundred with trade increasing sevenfold. As an army and navy base Bathurst was effective in stopping the slave trade. As a modest trading center it had begun well.

The man in charge of designing Bathurst in 1816 was Captain Alexander Grant of the British army. Captain Grant had earned his rank by fighting against Napoleon's forces in the important battle of Waterloo in Europe. Still brimming with pride he named the main streets of Bathurst after the victorious generals: Wellington, Picton, Anglesea, Blucher, Hill, Orange, and Cotton. But the neighborhoods that developed as the town grew were named after their principal occupants. Soldier Town was where discharged soldiers lived. Joloff Town was where the Wolofs from Senegal settled. Portuguese Town was where the mixed-blood descendants of previous European settlers dwelled. (The term "Portuguese" was used to refer to all *mulattoes*, people of mixed blood, no matter where their white ancestors had originally come from.) These residential neighborhoods were separated by strips of land where vegetable gardens were cultivated. The street pattern and many public buildings of the nineteenth century still stand today.

Unhealthy living conditions were a serious problem. Swamps to the south and west of the town not only brought high humidity and dampness but also mosquitoes. And the mosquitoes brought malaria. The mortality rates from malaria were extremely high. In

1825, for example, 199 soldiers arrived by ship. Of the 108 that moved into Banjul's barracks, 87 were dead by the end of that year's rainy season. The next year 200 more soldiers arrived as replacements from the British colony of Sierra Leone. Six months later 116 were still alive, but 93 were in the hospital under the care of a single doctor's assistant. Quinine, made from the bark of an Amazonian rain forest tree, had become known by then to protect against malaria, the biggest killer. But Europeans had not yet begun widespread use of quinine.

Another European group that suffered high casualty rates was the missionaries. The first group to arrive, the Wesleyan Methodist Mission of 1823, lost most of its members. The Quaker missionaries who arrived soon afterward returned to Britain, all except the one who had died of malaria or yellow fever (also transmitted by a mosquito). As a result their religious efforts met with little success outside the capital. Elsewhere Islam was steadily gaining converts.

It is difficult to understand why the whole settlement was not abandoned for a new one on the mainland. In 1859 yellow fever killed all the Europeans in Banjul except ten. A few years later one-fourth of the town's four thousand residents died from a cholera epidemic. This calamity gave one of Banjul's neighborhoods its name: Half Die. Such diseases were a regular feature of Banjul because of its swampy setting, which was worsened in the summer rainy season by street flooding. Mosquitoes could breed in the standing water. Urban transportation at these times was by rowboats. Sometimes a crocodile would wander in from the surrounding creeks, providing at least a bit of amusement. After the floods receded, city dwellers would experience healthier conditions.

Chapter 3

THE CIVIL WARS AND
THE BRITISH

The second half of the nineteenth century became yet another time of political turmoil in Gambian history. In distant parts of the Muslim world the conviction arose that Islam needed to become purer and gain more followers. This religious revival resulted in jihads that swept through Senegambia. Religious leaders, demanding religious, social, and political reforms, gained large followings among the people. They organized and attacked traditional rulers and groups who did not follow Islam. The result was fifty years of conflict called the Soninke-Marabout Wars.

THE SONINKE-MARABOUT WARS

Marabouts (the "t" is not pronounced) are Islamic religious teachers who traveled through West Africa for centuries establishing merchant communities among groups that were mostly animist. The religion of animism believes that human beings and nature exist in a special relationship in which people honor the environment by caring for it. Animists see nature as alive with deities in the rain, trees, and surroundings. The traditional animist kingdoms tolerated Muslim presence, and sometimes a non-Islamic ruler would hire a marabout who prayed for him, gave advice, and handled correspondence. In the first part of the nineteenth century most of the rulers and upper castes of kingdoms along the Gambia River were still not Muslims and did not have many Muslims among their subjects. These non-Muslim people came to be known as the Soninkes. They wished to continue their traditional beliefs and practices which included drinking alcoholic beverages, which is prohibited by Islam. Nor did they want to lose their power to religious leaders.

Slowly the power of Islam was spreading among the poor, who were most vulnerable to slavery–the lower castes. (The caste system reserves specific occupations for different social groups.) When the Atlantic slave trade had stopped, slavery continued within The Gambia, and those enslaved were placed into agricultural work. Villages populated by a Muslim majority organized themselves into a loose federation during the 1850s. Under marabout leadership they then declared a holy war against non-Muslims. During the first two decades of the war religious passion and duty motivated the marabouts and their lieutenants. Afterward it became less a religious crusade and more a struggle of certain leaders to gain power for themselves. In either case large armies were created. Great battles were fought. Villages were burned, and poor farmers and lower castes, who often found themselves caught in the middle without food reserves, suffered greatly. Once captured, they were forced to produce food surpluses for marabout factions.

The French and the British did not take sides in the struggle. The British made a special effort not to get involved, which shocked and disgusted the Soninke rulers who had enjoyed good relations with the British during and after the slave trade. Requests by Soninke kings for help from the British governor at Bathurst usually were denied. A problem that increased the turmoil even further was a series of annual invasions by yet another Islamic faction. These were thousands of Fula (also called Fulani, Fulbe, and Peul) warriors who invaded from the east and attacked both Soninke and Marabout villages. Famine spread as farmers abandoned their fields because they were too frightened to leave their villages and risk capture by warring factions.

The Europeans were unavoidably affected by the civil wars, but in different ways. In the French area of influence, growing peanuts for export had developed into a valuable business. Traders who bought these peanuts in the warring kingdoms demanded that French troops protect them. In both France and the Senegambia, French administrators dreamed of a future when most of West Africa would form part of an extensive French trading empire. Consequently, they used their limited military forces to defeat marabout leaders who became too powerful. They also built a series of forts to better control and protect the countryside for peanut cultivation.

The British Parliament, on the other hand, ordered their administrators not to get involved. The Soninke-Marabout War had interrupted trade along and around the Gambia River. British soldiers were to act only to avoid conflict or in situations when chances of creating a broader conflict were small. The civil wars in The Gambia lasted so long partly because the British government refused to take sides.

Toward the end of the nineteenth century the effects of the civil wars reached devastating proportions. Ethnic and family ties were broken when people became refugees and escaped to whatever place would accept them. People converted to Islam and changed their names, even their castes, to save their lives. Life became decentralized as kings lost their power to Muslim religious figures. Chiefs and the council of elders of each village took over leadership.

WHAT TO DO WITH THE GAMBIA

During the civil wars there were many years of negotiations between the French and the British over the Gambia River region. Both sides agreed that the British should receive a piece of French territory elsewhere in West Africa in exchange for their Gambia colony.

For several reasons this exchange did not take place. The local Gambian chiefs complained that they would have to start all over again after they had worked so hard to establish satisfactory relationships with the British. Gambians who had gone to missionary schools in Bathurst and the larger towns would lose their one advantage over other Gambians: their ability to speak and write English. The people living in the British area were vehemently opposed to French rule and made sure that the Parliament in London knew. The British merchants would lose their trade to Frenchmen. Wesleyan missionaries would be overpowered by French Catholic missionaries.

In 1885, following Belgium King Leopold's efforts to seize the Congo, the leading European nations sat down to carve up Africa among them. The British and French, together with smaller imperial European nations, made a sudden effort to grab as much

A painting of King Leopold II of Belgium

of unclaimed Africa as possible. The more colonies a European country had, the more potential mineral and agricultural resources it would exploit. As a result of this "Scramble for Africa," as historians call it, the British wondered whether they shouldn't keep their Gambian colony after all.

The British established a protectorate in 1888. It consisted of all the land along the Gambia River not within the three already established colonial areas: Bathurst; the Ceded Mile, a thin strip of land along the north riverbank opposite Bathurst; and MacCarthy Island, which was about 100 miles (161 kilometers) inland. This also was administered by the British, but separately. Also in 1888, administration of the Colony of The Gambia was separated from Sierra Leone and The Gambia given its own governor.

The following year, 1889, British and French delegates met in Paris. The Soninke-Marabout Wars had to be stopped so Britain and France could increase their potential profits in peanut cultivation. To avoid any conflict, they had to agree on the boundary between their territories. The British were more interested in expanding their empires in East Africa and South Africa. They therefore made no effort to demand from the French enough land to make The Gambia little more than a floodplain of the river. The idea of trading British Gambia for French land elsewhere in West Africa led nowhere, when the British decided the French offer was not satisfactory. As a result, nothing changed. The Anglo-French Convention of 1889 defined clearly the boundary of The Gambia, which, with some minor adjustments, is the same boundary that exists today: a country 14 to 30 miles (23 to 48 kilometers) wide and 192 miles (309 kilometers) long. The delegates who arranged this were convinced that this border was temporary. One day, they firmly believed, The Gambia would become part of French Senegal.

THE TWENTIETH CENTURY

Resistance by Gambians to British colonial rule was initially minimal. The Gambians were exhausted by more than 350 years of slave trade, 50 years of warfare, and years of disrupted agricultural production. In 1893 the British established a form of rule called "indirect rule" throughout the protectorate. This meant that the British would rule the area through "cooperating" Gambian chiefs rather than replacing the chiefs with Europeans. The British provided each chief with some financial support. Indirect rule also kept British administrative costs low. It was to remain the form of government in the protectorate until the country became independent in the 1960s.

The links between the chiefs and the British were two British officials called traveling commissioners. One was assigned the north bank of the river and the other the south bank. Their responsibility was to ensure that taxes were collected and to convey orders and requests to the chiefs. This became a critical

This engraving shows a British administrator of The Gambia at a reception of a native chief.

feature of colonial rule. Taxation forced farmers to spend more time growing peanuts for sale than growing their own food crops. Famines and food shortages became widespread during colonialism.

In Bathurst the central government of British Gambia made all laws and regulations for both the colony and the protectorate. This government consisted of the governor, appointed legislative and executive councils, the secretariat, and departments such as agriculture and public works. The closer ties between the two parts of British Gambia, the colony and the protectorate, meant new responsibilities for the British administration. All administrative costs were paid for by profits from peanut exports.

Economic development in The Gambia during the first fifty years was virtually nonexistent. British policy was that colonies should pay their own way. They certainly could not expect to be supported by the British treasury. There was a hut tax on all

Roads and potable water were among the improvements made by the British.

males and their dependents. This tax had to be paid in cash, and the only way to get cash was to grow peanuts. But producers received low prices from British traders. As this was totally insufficient, The Gambia remained poor and underdeveloped.

By the 1920s anticolonial sentiment was very high in British Africa. Then the Depression of the 1930s increased suffering and caused even greater problems. In 1942, in response to the growing demand for political independence and also because the Europeans needed Africans for soldiers in World War II, the British promised to provide development funds, but most of it never materialized. Some improvements were made in Bathurst. Some streets were paved, a hospital was built, and the port was upgraded. But the opportunity to build a successful airport that would attract flights from all over the world was lost to Dakar in French Senegal. Schemes to develop commercial egg and rice production on a large scale ended disastrously. Educational opportunities improved only because missionary groups helped out by establishing and maintaining elementary and secondary schools. The protectorate, almost all of what is today rural Gambia, was largely ignored.

British colonies were involved to some extent in both world wars. During World War I, four hundred Gambians fought with other colonial troops against the Germans in other parts of Africa. In World War II a few Gambian soldiers helped defend faraway Burma against the Japanese.

World War II marked the beginning of the end of Europe's colonial-based empires throughout the world. After the war the Europeans, both victors and vanquished, were too devastated to stifle the growing demand of their colonies for political independence. Educated Africans who had watched Europeans fight for freedom and helped them win the struggle against authoritarian countries, realized that the moment had arrived for independence from foreign rule. Africans were no longer to be treated as subjects. They had the right to rule themselves.

In a movement almost as sudden as the European scramble for Africa, independence swept Africa. In 1945 there were only four self-governing African states. By 1976 there were forty-seven. Among the British colonies of West Africa, Ghana demanded and got independence in 1957, Nigeria in 1960, and Sierra Leone in 1961. By 1961 all of West Africa was independent except for two colonies: Portuguese Guinea-Bissau and The Gambia. What had been the oldest, smallest, and poorest British colony in West Africa was now also Britain's last. The Gambia became formally independent in 1965.

The shift to independence was gradual. In the 1950s various constitutions increased the number of Gambians on the legislative council. These members were elected, not appointed by the British. The constitution of 1960 created a thirty-four-member House of Representatives. Seven seats were for representatives of the colony and twelve were for the protectorate. Of this last group only eight were selected by the chiefs rather than through popular elections. This meant that the chiefs had lost more of their power.

There was heavy voter participation in the election of 1960. Voters could pick from the People's Progressive party, the United party, and the Democratic Congress Alliance. The result, a stalemate, was so unsatisfactory to all the political groups that another constitution was written. The 1962 constitution gave Gambians full self-rule, and the protectorate chiefs lost virtually all their power. As a result of the 1962 elections, the leader of the People's Progressive party, David Jawara, became prime minister.

Despite continuing doubts as to The Gambia's capacity for survival as an independent country, talks with the British to set a date of complete independence were begun. On February 18, 1965, The Gambia became an independent state within the Commonwealth, a group of ex-British colonies that still accepted the British monarch as symbolic leader. Unlike other African countries that Africanized their names after achieving independence, The Gambia kept its name, which was African already. On April 24, 1970, following the wishes of the Gambian people, The Gambia left the Commonwealth and became a republic, a democratic country that does not have a monarch as actual or symbolic leader. David or Dauda Jawara, who subsequently converted to Islam, now called Sir David Jawara, became the country's first president.

An Independence Day celebration

Chapter 4

THE NATION OF

THE GAMBIA

THE GOVERNMENT

The Gambia is a republic. It has an executive branch consisting of a president, vice-president, and a cabinet. The president is elected every five years. The legislative branch is the House of Representatives with fifty members. Thirty-five representatives are elected directly by the voters every five years; five are elected by the tribal chiefs, four are nominees, and six are presidential appointees. The Gambia's civil service, the government employees, has been described as one of the best and most efficient in Africa.

The Gambia is one of the few African countries with a real multiparty system in which citizens actually have the power to make political changes. This is partly because there is not much to disagree about. The only issues have been whether to become a republic and how close their ties with Senegal should be.

There are three main political parties. The People's Progressive party (PPP) has won the majority of seats in the House of Representatives since independence. It mainly represents the rural areas that were the protectorate. Its greatest supporters are the Mandinkas, the most important group in the country. Another party is the Gambia People's party (GPP). The third is the National Convention party (NCP), the main opposition party.

Banjul, the capital, is run by an elected town council. The remainder of the country is divided into six more council areas: Kombo Saint Mary, Western, North Bank, Lower River, MacCarthy Island, and Upper River. Each council is proportionately funded and is responsible for local government services. Chiefs retain power over traditional activities in the smaller governing units called districts, of which there are thirty-five.

The political process in The Gambia is just and law-abiding. For example, a popular referendum was held in 1970 to determine whether the people wished The Gambia to become a republic or not. This referendum was hailed by world leaders as one that was just and fair. The Gambia has become known as a country of secret balloting and honest elections. Civil rights and personal liberties are protected.

DAUDA JAWARA, PROMINENT LEADER

If there is one person who has been identified with The Gambia as an independent country, it is Sir Dauda Kairaba Jawara. He was prime minister from 1962 to 1970 and has been president since 1970. No one has had a more important role in making the country what it is today.

Jawara was born in 1924 in the upriver Mandinka village of Barajally. His father was a prosperous farmer and trader. Because education was so expensive for a farming family, he was the only one of six children to be sent to school in Bathurst. He attended a Muslim primary school. Later he was accepted at the Methodist Boys High School, the only high school that existed then. In all of his classes Jawara was number one. After graduating he joined the colonial medical department as a male nurse at the Royal Victorian Hospital.

Two years later he decided to become a veterinarian and left The Gambia to study in the West African country of Ghana and later at the Veterinary School at Glasgow University in Scotland. While in Glasgow he began to show interest in politics: he joined the African Students Union and became its president. In 1954 he returned to The Gambia as a veterinary officer for the agriculture department.

For most of the next six years, Jawara inspected and inoculated cattle and taught the farmers to improve their breeds. He once said, many years later, that "There's not a cow in The Gambia that doesn't know me personally." He became the chief veterinary officer. He converted to Christianity and took the name David. Having come this far from being a village boy, Jawara married a daughter of the most important and cultivated family of the capital.

Jawara returned to politics. He helped form the People's Progressive party in 1959 and was chosen its leader. When The Gambia became independent in 1965, Jawara became prime minister. He also returned to the Muslim faith and changed his name from David back to Dauda.

Jawara has become well known for his continuing efforts to call

Sir Dauda Jawara

attention to the problems of the environment and the need to conserve Africa's resources. In 1980 he was awarded a medal by the Food and Agriculture Organization of the United Nations for his efforts to lessen the destructive impact of droughts. He banned charcoal production that contributed to deforestation and wasted fuel and wood.

Jawara is a shy, quiet, and courteous man. He takes his work seriously, working at home as much as at the office. His leadership was one of the most important factors that allowed The Gambia to become independent when it did. Since then his leadership has been decisive in keeping his country independent and peaceful.

THE REVOLUTION OF 1981

The Gambia's peaceful path since achieving independence has been interrupted only once. In the revolution of 1981, Banjul was damaged and President Jawara almost lost his power and position.

Until 1981 The Gambia was one of the few countries of Africa without political prisoners and with almost no cases of murder or suicide. (For this reason, The Gambia was selected to be the site of the Organization of African Unity's Summit on Human Rights in 1980.) The Gambia had no army. After the British left, the only military personnel was a branch of the police called The Gambia field force. It had only five hundred men.

But in the late 1970s all was not well. There was unhappiness among the men of the field force, who believed the president no longer trusted them. They believed the administration and ruling party (the PPP) had become lazy and corrupt. The government was criticized by young people as one that thought only of helping itself. These young people created small political parties that demanded change through revolution. Some groups resented what they believed to be too many government favors to Jawara's dominant ethnic group, the Mandinka. Moreover, farmers in the countryside were upset about the weak government response to the continuing drought that hurt agriculture.

In July 1981 President Jawara went to London to represent his country at the wedding of Prince Charles and Princess Diana. While he was there, on July 30, members of the field force seized the arsenal, opened the gates to the prison, and marched on Banjul. They seized the radio station and announced to the people that there now was a new government led by "The Revolutionary Council of Twelve." By that evening all of Banjul except the central police station, all nearby roads, and the ferry to the north bank of the river were controlled by the rebels. They also had taken one hundred hostages, among them President Jawara's wife

In Great Britain in 1987 President Jawara (first left) was seated with (left to right) Prince Philip, Canadian Prime Minister Brian Mulroney, Queen Elizabeth II, and Zambian President Kenneth Kaunda.

and four of his children. That same morning, as soon as he received the news in London, President Jawara made arrangements to fly to Dakar. Relying on a 1967 defense treaty, help was requested from the Senegalese government. During the next three days six hundred Senegalese troops captured Yundum Airport, the roads, the ferry, and then Banjul itself. Jawara returned to Banjul on the last day. The hostages were released unharmed two days later.

The revolution had several long-term effects. One was closer ties between Senegal and The Gambia for several years. On December 29, 1981, the legislatures of both countries signed a treaty creating the Confederation of the Senegambia. Senegal's president became its president, and President Jawara was the vice-president. Though the Gambians were against unification, President Jawara believed he owed this attempt to the Senegalese who had stopped the revolution for him. Nevertheless, with the passing of time the impact of the revolution lessened. The Gambia's interest in the confederation also dwindled. The confederation today exists mainly on paper.

Because the revolution clearly indicated that the field force was no longer trustworthy, a major effort had to be made to replace it. Permanent dependence on the Senegalese army for police duties and protection in The Gambia was certainly not welcome by either the government or the people.

With the help of British army advisers, a Gambian national army was created. In the 1980s it consisted of 450 soldiers, 150 of whom were in the Senegal-Gambia confederated battalion. Another change was the creation of the Gambian rural police, modeled after the rural police force of Senegal. It patrols the countryside, but Banjul and the towns are under the jurisdiction of a separate police force.

Despite the revolution, The Gambia has returned to its world of peace and respect for law and justice. While murder and treason are now punishable by death, the president can commute these sentences to life imprisonment and he regularly does so. All but one of the men convicted of treason for their participation in the 1981 revolution have had their sentences changed to life imprisonment.

FOREIGN RELATIONS

The relationship The Gambia has with other countries is determined largely by location and past history. The Gambia has especially close relations with Great Britain, Senegal, and African states that once were British colonies. The Gambia follows a moderate pro-Western policy in international affairs. This means

The Gambia's minister for foreign affairs, Omar B. Sey, (seated behind nameplate) attends a meeting of the United Nations General Assembly in 1993.

the wealthy and powerful countries of North America and Europe are considered friends. The Gambia's main forums for expressing opinions and contacting other states are the United Nations and the Organization of African Unity.

The only issue of great importance relating to other states is that of the union with larger and more populous Senegal. After 1982, when the treaty of confederation was signed, relations were especially close between the two countries. Various joint Gambia-Senegal working groups existed in certain government departments. But by the early 1990s cooperation had collapsed. Border conflicts and continued unresolvable disagreements are reasons given for this. Nevertheless, because The Gambia is almost totally surrounded by Senegal, her relationship with that country will always be of the greatest importance.

The Gambia has been active in African and Arab affairs. During

Gambian troops helped to enforce a cease-fire in Liberia in 1990.

the war between Iran and Iraq from 1981 to 1988, President
Jawara served as the chair of the Islamic Peace Conference that
tried to end the bloodshed between these Muslim states. Toward
the end of the Liberian civil war of 1990, The Gambia's army
went to that West African country, together with other West
African armies, to try to stop the violence. Although they were
not successful, it is a good example of The Gambia's desire to
actively participate with other African countries to bring about
positive change.

Finally, under President Jawara's leadership, The Gambia has
become a champion of protection of the environment and of the
need to preserve human rights. The Gambia is the headquarters of
the African Commission on Human Rights. In 1993 The Gambia
was the site of the World Conference on Human Rights.

Gambian schoolgirls

EDUCATION

Education in The Gambia suffers from the same problems found in other poor countries of the world – an area often called the Third World. In such countries children are important to the economic well-being of the family. Children often take care of cattle, help in farming, or take care of younger brothers, sisters, and cousins. To send a child to school is an expensive sacrifice. As a result, one out of every three children of school age never attend. The number of adults who can read and write are only about 27 percent of the population.

Becoming educated is certainly more difficult for rural children than for those who live in Banjul. In The Gambia children who live in the villages and small towns find going to school difficult and certainly something unusual. If they are needed at home or in the fields they may miss school for weeks.

61

The child at the left in the back is holding a copy of the Qur'an.

High school students

This does not mean that Gambians are not educated. Everyone in a village learns the myths, lore, history, skills, and knowledge that are required to function as an adult. All children learn prayers and part of the Qur'an, the holy book of Islam. The best will go to special Islamic schools and will learn to read Arabic, the language in which the Qur'an is written.

To have a high school diploma is a great achievement for a Gambian. Foreigners living in the country, such as British and Lebanese, send their sons and daughters abroad for their schooling. Gambians would like to do the same, but most can't afford it. The Gambia is one of the few countries in Africa without a university. There is a two-year teacher-training school called Yundum College. To go to a university the Gambian student needs a full scholarship, but only a dozen or so are available each year.

Banjul is the largest city in The Gambia and the center of banking (inset).

Banjul

Chapter 5

BANJUL AND THE COAST

BANJUL

Banjul is the seat of government, the center of banking and commerce, an underused port, and a small city with diverse inhabitants. One can still find signs in the distant rural areas at the other end of the country that refer to it by its British name, Bathurst. The Gambian name Banjul became official in 1973.

Banjul is a city that is quaint, small, homely, and rather jolly. It resembles cities of the Caribbean. Typical Banjul buildings are two stories high with shops on street level and living quarters above. They have shaded courtyards, entered through open wooden or stucco gateways. Building walls are pastel colored in pink, blue, or cream. On top are corrugated tin, pagoda-style roofs. Picturesque bungalows that survive from the British period are English architectural styles adapted to the tropics with balconies, shutters, and dormer windows. They are raised on pillars to

Brightly colored fabrics (inset) and ready-made women's clothing (above) are for sale in the market in Banjul.

improve air circulation and minimize flooding. From the streets one can observe interesting arches, lattices, and verandas. From these buildings one can see flowering trees and the hustle and bustle of vivid street life.

The focus of much of the city's life is the Albert Market near the river. Winding lanes full of color burst with activity. The stalls along the lanes sell local and imported products such as clothes, beads, kola nuts, tresses to be braided into the hair, tea, and fruit. Lanes that specialize in clothing sell tie-dyed dresses, robes, and shirts. Hand-painted T-shirts are much in demand. Elsewhere Lebanese merchants have stalls with rolls of bright, patterned cloth from which the Gambians fashion clothing that dazzles with color.

The Albert Market, like street corners throughout the city, is also populated by food vendors. Women sit behind rows of large

People in Banjul do their grocery shopping at colorful street markets (left), or at regular supermarkets (above).

bowls filled with a variety of delicious, spicy cooked dishes that can be served with rice or on a piece of fresh bread. A Gambian specialty is *benachin*, fish stewed with vegetables and served with rice. Another is *damoda*, peanut sauce stew with meat and vegetables. This is the African version of inexpensive, but nutritious, fast food.

Though Banjul is far from being a wealthy town, it does not have the extremes found in other capitals. Crushing poverty and ugly slums are not found here. The poor live in relatively clean one-room wood or tin houses clustered around dirt courtyards. Such a group of houses is called a compound. The women do the cooking and clothes washing at the compound's one water tap, which draws on a system that provides water clean enough for drinking. Families living in a compound are usually related or at least from the same village. They help each other financially.

The people of Banjul are friendly and relaxed.

Because they all make little money, they pool their efforts to survive. Many are in debt to the Mauritanian or Lebanese shopkeepers.

Perhaps the real wealth of Banjul and of The Gambia is its people. The visitor is struck by their friendly demeanor, their kindness and hospitality, and their good nature. They are certainly open and relaxed, compared with the inhabitants of some other capital cities. In the street, everyone stops to chat with friends. People are courteous and have plenty of time for each other. Introductions that begin all conversations are elaborate and lengthy. This creates a small-town atmosphere where the pace of life is relaxed and there is a feeling of closeness and belonging.

This closeness and informality affects even the workings of the government. It is not unheard-of to have a visit with a government official while he is shopping on Wellington Street or

Many people, especially the women, wear traditional clothing.

relaxing in the lounge of the Atlantic Hotel. A citizen can sometimes call and make an appointment to see the president the same day.

Banjul has a diverse ethnic mix. There are Aku (descendants of slaves recaptured on the high seas by the British after the trade was abolished in 1807 and who were resettled in freedom), Fula (pastoralists), Jola (from the river's south bank, who fiercely resisted slavery), Mandinka (the dominant rural ethnic group), Serrahuli (long-distance merchant traders), Serer (fishers and salt traders), and Wolofs (dominant in the capital's intellectual and artistic life). From other countries have come petty traders, which include Mauritanian Muslims known as Moors and Guineans. Farmers and farm laborers come chiefly from Guinea-Bissau and Mali. Major businesses are organized by Lebanese and government advisers, and development experts are principally Europeans on two- to four-year contracts.

Some of the handmade
crafts available in
The Gambia are wood
carvings and jewelry.

Though it may not be obvious on a map, Banjul was built on an island. What appears to be land to the west are salty mudflats and mangrove swamps, often underwater. A single road with a bridge leads out of the city across the swamp to link Banjul with the rest of the country.

Because of this physical limitation Banjul has not been able to expand. As a result, a series of suburbs have grown up at a distance on the mainland. In a way, time has left Banjul behind. Compared to the settlements on the mainland, the capital appears to be a living museum with its quaint houses, colorful markets, and British colonial flavor. The new suburbs are modern, though not necessarily much more comfortable or attractive. On the river's south bank and along the Atlantic coast, at Bakau and Fajara, are the residences of the wealthy. Here are the embassies and the hotels with their swimming pools, water sports, and evening entertainments. The president's residence is here, and so are all the businesses that flourish where there are tourists: restaurants, bike rental shops, and stores that sell Gambian handmade crafts.

Farther inland, in the suburb of Serekunda, are the homes of poorer Gambians and migrants from neighboring countries who cannot fit into Banjul. In the 1990s Serekunda's population passed that of the capital by a considerable degree.

THE COAST

The Gambia's coast, short as it is, is the center of the country's fishing and tourism industries. The coast is known for beaches that are described as slices of paradise. They are curved, with cliffs jutting into the ocean at either end. These headlands provide

Left: Tourists from England and Scandinavia escape the winter cold by vacationing on the beaches in The Gambia. Above: Tourists enjoy a barbecue dinner at a hotel.

wonderful views of the brilliant, white coral sand and the deep green, curving border of coconut palms. A sea of brilliant blue stretches under a blue sky. Giant waves explode against the beach. Not visible are the fierce currents that make swimming dangerous. A steep drop-off of the shore beneath the water and a powerful undertow can pull bathers out to sea. Despite this limitation, the natural beauty, together with miserable winter weather conditions in Europe, brings as many as 100,000 tourists, year after year, from as far away as Scandinavia.

Hotels that line the northern end of the coast vary in size, quality, and charm. Some belong to international hotel chains. Their bars are popular, but so are their pools, their gardens, and the stages where entertainment is provided. Tourists wander away from the hotels and beaches to eat at nearby restaurants or to visit tourist markets where they are offered hand-carved African masks, batik clothes, and peanuts. When not shopping or sunbathing, tourists can be found skimming down the coast

Bird-watchers use binoculars to observe the great variety of birdlife which is found everywhere, including hotel patios.

avenue on mopeds, bicycles, and dune scooters. Because The Gambia is a bird-watcher's paradise, some may be seen attempting to catch a glimpse of The Gambia's forest birds or the many seabirds and waders.

What makes the beaches so attractive is that they are generally deserted. Occasionally, a herd of big-horned white cattle will come to lick the salt on the rocks. More frequently there are fishers returning from or leaving for work. Behind the line of coconut palms there are lagoons, mangroves, and a village now and then. Then the wooded bushland begins and stretches east to the end of the country.

The small villages that dot the coast are the homes of fishing people. Each village has its own strip of beach and its own

Carving a pirogue

collection of *pirogues*. Pirogues are long, narrow, double-prowed dugout canoes made from wood. Pirogues are still built by hand with great care. They vary in size from 6.5 to 66 feet (2 to 20 meters) and are painted bright colors. The prows have a knifelike shape. Though narrow, pirogues are wide enough for two paddlers positioned side by side. They have a flat bottom and high sides. A space in the middle is reserved for the net and the fish that have been caught.

Even though many use simple equipment, the Gambian fishers have at their front doors some of the best fishing waters of the Atlantic. They catch small shrimp, lobsters, and fish such as wrasse, flying fish, yellowtail, snapper, saltwater catfish, rock hind, mullet, sea bream, dorado, and mackerel tuna. In the bottom of the pirogues the fish sparkle with color in the strong tropical sunshine.

A young man prepares fish for smoking (left). Oysters are cooked over a fire (right).

At the smaller villages the fish caught feed the fishers and their families. Because of the tourist boom of recent decades, these villagers also pick up a little extra income. They sell some of the fish to the tourists for beach barbecues. They also provide dancers to entertain at night on the beach where torches have been set up.

The exception is the fishing town of Gunjar, which has been modernized by the government and so is not of interest to tourists. Gunjar fishers have a small fleet of specially designed fishing boats that are powered by outboard motors instead of oars and sails. There are special smoking ovens and fish freezers. Instead of being carried by women with baskets on their heads, the fish are transported to the rest of the country by truck. Some small fish are salted for use in local dishes.

A small village

Chapter 6

RURAL LIFE AND
RELIGION

The Gambia has a large rural population. In the mid-1980s, approximately 77 percent of Gambians lived in villages where the main occupation was agriculture.

THE SETTLEMENT PATTERN

It might be expected that many of The Gambia's towns and villages would be located along the dominant physical feature of the country–the Gambia River. But because of flooding and the importance of peanut production the opposite is true. Generally speaking, the dominant settlement pattern is a ribbon of occupied land, parallel to the river, located either just outside the floodplain or farther away from the river on the uplands. There are two such ribbons: one north of the river, one to the south. Each stretches east and west from one end of the country to the other.

The typical village site is on the rising slope between the river's swamplands below and the higher, dry uplands slightly above. This location minimizes the risk from flooding. It also gives them equal access to both the flat, swampy land (called *banta faros*), where they grow rice, bananas, and vegetables and collect palm oil for cooking, and to the rain-fed uplands, which are favorable for growing peanuts, cotton, millet, and sorghum.

Changing transport patterns also explain this settlement pattern. The river, of course, was the only transportation route for centuries. So along the river's banks are more than thirty uninhabited landings where boats can load and unload. These are connected to the villages by dirt trails that run at right angles to the river. The villages are usually about five miles (eight kilometers) from the closest river landing. However, in the last fifty years road transport has become important as well. The north bank road and the south bank road connect many of the villages. Because of the location of the villages, a traveler crossing The Gambia by road rarely sees the river. The main exceptions to this settlement pattern are Georgetown and Basse, which are situated on the banks of the Gambia River.

VILLAGE STRUCTURE

A typical village sits in a landscape of concentric land use circles. Trees and uncultivated bush stick out above the tall millet and sorghum crops. Scattered among a clump of baobab and silk cotton trees, weathered screens made of millet stalks and the orange of rusting iron roofs indicate the presence of a village.

A village is formed by a large number of compounds. Each

The interior of a village compound

compound is a series of huts or houses grouped together around a large open space. All of this is surrounded by a fence made of tall reeds laced by rope made from the baobab bark. A compound contains the houses of an extended family: a group who share descent from a common male ancestor. When a woman marries, she moves to her husband's compound. A compound carries the name of its founder or of the family and includes the man and wife, their sons with their wives and children, and unmarried daughters. The compound of the Bajo family would be referred to as the *Bajo Kunda*. Some families are more cohesive than others with everyone getting along. Others, where harmony isn't achieved, may split up into smaller units.

In front of this building, the corrugated roof extends over a veranda to provide shade.

More prosperous villages have houses made of concrete, with tin roofs, while poorer villages have houses with mud walls. The unplastered mud walls have long vertical cracks created by weather conditions. There are no windows: the light enters from the doorway and through gaps where the roof beams sit on the walls (the favorite entrance of mosquitoes in the wet season). The beds are made from branches held up by forked posts stuck in the rocky floor. Ghostly white mosquito nets hang above them. The only furniture is mats, wood chests, and a clay water jar.

Some roofs are constructed of brittle, gray thatch that inevitably lets in the rain. Corrugated iron roofs are rainproof but get hot in the midday sun. Some homes have verandas in front supported by twisted posts. Animals are not allowed inside the houses except for the occasional chicken who might enter without being noticed. Sheep and goats are tethered outside in the courtyard and cattle are kept in nearby fields.

Screens made of millet stalks or braided bamboo are used for privacy.

Each part of the extended family has its own house and courtyard and each wife has her own dwelling that she shares with her children. Privacy for interior courts is provided by screens of millet stalks or braided bamboo across the entrance.

The larger spaces between compound walls could be called streets. Many lanes branch off these streets to smaller compounds farther back. The streets and lanes are of pale, gold sand spotted and stained by ashes and animal droppings. During the day, when everyone is out in the fields, only children and a few elderly people wander through the compounds and streets, ignoring the dogs that slowly move about in the hard, white light.

The main streets eventually widen into a large space that is the village meeting place. Here is the *bantaba*, a raised platform of logs constructed under the village's main shade tree. Here the men come when they are not working to sit, talk, and pass the time of day. The shape and construction of the bantaba are such that air can pass below to help cool its users. Nearby will be the simple village mosque, the Muslim house of worship.

VILLAGE LIFE

It is apparent from the design of a village that strong family ties are important to the Gambians. The wealthier members help support poorer relatives, no matter what the personal relations between them may be or how difficult the circumstances. People are judged not on how wealthy they are but on how well they treat their kin. Besides belonging to a family and to a village, rural Gambians are linked to non-family members through hereditary occupations (castes) and work groups organized by age and sex to help families in need or provide a large labor force for community work projects.

The chief and the village headman are drawn from the original families that founded the village. In the nineteenth century when they enjoyed more power and independence from government officials, each chief (*alkalo*, *alkali*, or *alkab*), had forty or more assistants. Today a chief has from two to six assistants. The government pays the chief a small salary and pension. The chief's duties are concerned with village-government relations.

The headman, *sate-tio*, is in charge of keeping order and justice within the village. Traditionally his name is not told to outsiders. He is the oldest member of the village's most important family. When he dies, the older villagers choose one of his brothers or sons to be the new sate-tio.

The cora *is a stringed instrument with a gourd bottom.*

Another important person is the *imam*, the chief religious leader. He leads prayers on Fridays and is responsible for teaching about Islam to the young people.

The historian of the village is the griot, who is attached to a prominent family. The griot communicates local history, genealogies, and village social structure. This information is not written down but is recorded in memory and communicated orally. Stories are accompanied by drumming and playing the *cora*, a stringed instrument with a gourd bottom that produces harplike sounds. Even today, influential men are praised by their family's griots on important occasions. Because griots all belong to an especially low caste, they are not allowed to be buried with everyone else.

All but the extremely old and young in the village are farmers. Land is owned by the village and divided among the families in the compound. Usually there is enough land for everyone in the village. The soil in the tropics is not fertile and buying fertilizer is far too expensive, so individual fields cannot be cultivated for many years in a row. When the soil in a field becomes less fertile, it is used for cattle rearing and other fields are cleared for farming. The cattle manure fertilizes the soil and enables the farmer to plant there again a few years later. If a family moves away, use of their land is given to another family.

Work is organized by dividing the village people into groups according to sex and then again according to age. Adults between eighteen and forty do heavy work such as building roads, digging wells, and farm work. The elders make decisions for the village and supervise work. In recent years, however, so many young adults have moved to the towns that the elderly often must work too. Men are given the responsibility of growing crops for cash sale (peanuts and cotton) and for eating (millet, sorghum, corn, and sometimes manioc). Men also are required to keep the compounds in good condition by reroofing, refencing digging new latrines, and so forth.

Women cultivate rice and vegetables in the lowland swamps and care for the poultry. They haul water from the well, pound grain, cook, do housework, and care for the children. Girls help their mothers and aunts care for the infants and do housework. Boys herd animals and help the women collect firewood.

Because of the dependence on agriculture, the life of the village is closely tied to the seasons. The green, rainy season is the season of tremendous agricultural activity. Fields must be prepared, planted, and tended. Because everything grows so

*After pirogues have brought in the fish,
women cut and clean the catch.*

quickly, weeding is a never-ending job. The weeks before the harvest are called the "hungry season," because all the grain and cash saved since the last harvest are in short supply or gone.

The dry season begins with the harvest and the sale of the peanuts. When the harvest is over people can relax. This is the time when villagers organize the annual initiation ceremonies for young people who are passing into adulthood. There are other village celebrations as well. Projects such as repairing roofs and making textiles, pottery, and tools are taken care of during the dry season. This is also a time for visiting relatives and looking for other types of work to increase the family's income.

The diet of the villagers, like the diet of most poor people of the world, is essentially a grain that is consumed at every meal, every day. Variety is achieved by adding a little of something that has a strong taste to it. A typical dish is a porridge of rice or millet that is made more interesting with the addition of a thin, spicy peanut sauce. Corn and sorghum are the other grains consumed. Gambians eat rice with dried fish and pounded raw peanuts, rice with palm oil, and rice with a sauce of fish, tomatoes, and chili peppers. Whatever the food, it is served from large bowls and eaten by cupping the food in the right hand and bringing it to one's mouth.

WOMEN

The women of The Gambia, like the women of most of sub-Saharan Africa and many other poor parts of the world, are the bulwark of society. They are the work force of the nation, working terribly hard, day after day, in a difficult swampy environment to produce most of the food that feeds the populace. But compared to Gambian men, the lifestyle options they have are limited. They are seldom educated, and few opportunities exist to earn cash. Nevertheless, visitors are struck by their endurance, their gaiety, and their pride in their family and community. Vibrant, energetic, expressive, and dressed with flair, Gambian women ensure the continuity of life and hope in their society.

Only recently has the importance of women in developing countries become appreciated. Some experts believe that the single most important change that should be made to help relieve poverty in many countries is to increase the quality and quantity of formal education received by girls and women. This is true for The Gambia too, where fewer than 10 percent of females are literate.

While men make all the important decisions at the village and compound levels, women exercise power collectively through their *kafos*. A kafo is a village group formed of women of a similar age.

Gambian women belong to support groups called kafos.

It functions as a woman's social security network. If one member falls sick during a critical agricultural period, her kafo members will ensure that her fields are managed. Each kafo is formed when the women are young and survives until they are too old to have a role in society. All the girls of the village born within a five- to ten-year period belong to the same kafo. The kafo sometimes even controls fields and plots for cash crops. In recent years with foreign funding, some kafos have begun to grow sesame and vegetables for income. Together the members make decisions about the cultivation of these fields. The kafo keeps any profit from the sale of crops it has grown to be used as a fund to assist members who may have a medical emergency. Kafo work and earnings are a Gambian woman's insurance fund. They choose a leader, they work together, and they support each other in times of personal crisis.

The woman on the left wears a caftan and the other wears a blouse and faneau.

Many men wear caftans.

DRESS

Gambians of both sexes prefer loose-fitting clothing in which the shape of the body is not obvious. This tradition comes from the Muslim belief that the human body should not be displayed. It is also more comfortable in hot weather because it keeps the body cooler. Men wear *caftans* or *warambas*, long gowns with elongated armholes, over baggy trousers.

Women too wear caftans. But more typical is a blouse and a *faneau*. The faneau is a piece of cloth tied at the waist to form a skirt. In Gambian society the legs of a woman, especially the thighs, must never be exposed in public. Shawls are worn around the shoulders at night when the temperature gets cooler. Women rarely go bareheaded–again, for religious reasons. Usually a cloth is attractively wrapped around the head to form a type of turban. Inexpensive rubber sandals, flip-flops, are on everyone's feet. In Banjul and the larger towns, men and women often wear Western-style clothing.

Drums are played during celebrations.

DRUMS AND DANCE

As in much of Africa, music in The Gambia means the beating of drums. Drums are often the only musical instrument played. Drums are so important that traditionally they are considered sacred, to be played only under carefully controlled circumstances. For example, a harvest celebration is considered a valid reason to play drums. To play drums just for the sake of playing them is considered inappropriate.

The beating of drums is accompanied by dancing or hand clapping or both. Each rhythm has a special meaning. For example, one rhythm exists for men, another for women. Despite their heavy burdens in agriculture and homemaking, women dance much more than men. And they usually dance by themselves. A drum beats a rhythm, friends clap their hands and whistle, and a woman jumps into the middle of the circle of

Women dancing (left) and a young man (right) selling cassettes of popular music

people. Dancing for about a minute, by herself or with others, she stamps her feet on the bare ground and thrusts her arms into the air. Her body expresses total, uncontrollable energy in which every single muscle is used. Then she melts into the admiring crowd and another woman takes her place to repeat the same enjoyable experience.

While drumming remains important, new, popular music has appeared in recent times. This is played by nonhereditary, professional musicians who use other traditional instruments such as a harp-lute, a wooden gourd, and a xylophone. These musicians are frequently Senegalese but, thanks to radio and cassettes, are well known in The Gambia.

Of course, when the young people of the village or town get together at night and dance for fun, they do not use such an important instrument as a drum. Instead, they turn on their boom boxes and play disco music. African pop and reggae from the West Indies are especially popular.

ISLAM

Ninety percent of Gambians are Muslims, most of them converted during the Soninke-Marabout Wars in the nineteenth century. The remainder are Christian (Aku and Jola) or animist (chiefly Jola). *Islam* is an Arabic word meaning "submission to the will of God. " Those who follow Islam are called Muslims. Islam's founder, an Arab named Muhammad, was born around A.D. 570. When Muhammad was forty he claimed to have received information from God. He started preaching, emphasizing always the idea that there is only one God and that people should stop worshiping idols. Eventually Muhammad became a military as well as a religious leader. He died in A.D. 632.

No religion has ever spread so rapidly. Within fifty years Islam reached as far west as the Atlantic coast of North Africa and as far east as the islands of Indonesia on the edge of the Pacific. North African traders following ancient trans-Sahara trade routes brought Islam to West Africa.

Like Christianity and Judaism, Islam has its holy book. It is called the Qur'an and is almost always written in Arabic. It has two parts. One is the word of God (*Allah*), as revealed to Muhammad in a series of statements. The other part consists of interpretations of Muhammad's actions at certain moments during his lifetime.

Islam is not just a religion, it is a way of life. It requires five daily prayers, Friday mosque attendance, and the giving of 10 percent of one's income, the *zakat*, for charity.

The core of Islam is the Five Pillars, the five acts that demonstrate the believer's faith. All Muslims must try to fulfill these. The first is to state "There is no God but Allah and

A mosque in Banjul (left) and a small village mosque (right)

Muhammad is his Prophet." The second is to pray five times each day while facing the holy Arab city of Mecca in Saudi Arabia. The third pillar is to take part in the feast of Ramadan, a month in which there is no eating during daylight hours. Fourth is the necessity of the wealthy to help those who are poor. And fifth is to make a pilgrimage to Mecca at least once in a person's lifetime, if one can afford to do so. Those who have made this journey are allowed to add the title of *hajji* to their name and wear distinctive headgear. The president of The Gambia is one of these people.

Islam does not have priests but does have prayer leaders. There are also religious experts called *ulema* who explain and interpret the rules and regulations. A good Muslim is expected not to smoke, drink alcohol, eat pork, or gamble. Women, though they have rights, are considered inferior to men. The sexes are to mix socially as little as possible. A man may have up to four wives if he can afford to support them and their children.

RELIGION IN THE GAMBIA

Before Islam reached this part of Africa, the people were
animists. While most Gambians are Muslims, some of their pre-
Islamic beliefs still are practiced. This is especially true for rural
Gambians. They no longer worship their ancestors but they
believe, as they have for centuries, that in the eyes of God, their
village is sacred because of the nearby burial of ancestors who
protect the village from harm. Many continue to believe that the
world is inhabited by active gods and devils, sacred animals and
trees, and magical pools of water.

Many villagers also believe that unexplained events like bad
luck or sudden death are the work of witches. It is said that
witches steal people's souls when they are vulnerable to attack,
for example, immediately after being born or during circumcision.
Some Gambians believe as firmly in witches as some Americans
believe in flying saucers or ghosts.

A special characteristic of West African Islam is the marabouts.
These men are the former witch-doctor healers who with
conversion have become a combination of priest, sage, prophet,
and mystic. At one time they were the only people who could
read and write. Because they were the only ones who could know
what was in the Qur'an, they were considered to have powers
that bordered on the magical. Because of their influence over the
people the government treats them with special consideration.

Typical of the blending of Islamic and non-Islamic religious
beliefs is the wearing of *jujus*. A juju is a leather amulet worn
around the wrist, neck, waist, or ankle to bring good luck. For
many West Africans the Qur'an is not simply a book of religious
information but is, itself, an object of power. Pieces of this holy

book are believed to be capable of providing a human being with whatever he or she needs. But handwriting of the Qur'an's phrases is forbidden. Only the marabout knows which sections are permitted. The marabout will write a quote from the Qur'an on a piece of paper that is sewn inside a small envelope of leather. During the Soninke-Marabout Wars, warriors fighting with the marabouts wore jujus that they believed protected them from bullets, swords, or arrows. Today, Gambians believe that the medicine brought by white people has its beneficial uses, but only the juju is effective protection against the problems created by witches and devils. Jujus help in situations in which Americans might seek help from a psychologist.

The largest, most satisfying religious feast in The Gambia is *Tobaski*. It is held at the end of Ramadan, the traditional time that pilgrims to Mecca are supposed to return home. Savings are used to buy a sheep or goat that is slaughtered as a sacrifice to God. The imam must always kill his first. It is a time of giving. Those able to own and sacrifice send gifts of raw meat to their friends, to Muslim leaders, and to the poor and needy of their communities. For the poor, Tobaski might be the only time of the year when they eat meat.

In general, Islam is observed faithfully. There is little drinking of alcohol. Large numbers of people attend the mosque each Friday and the majority pray five times a day after ritually washing themselves. At government offices, private shops, in peanut fields, or at the river's edge, everything stops while the Gambians turn toward the direction of Mecca and kneel on straw mats. They hold prayer beads between their fingers and touch their foreheads to the ground. Throughout the country people chant, "There is no god but Allah, and Muhammad is his prophet."

A holy communion procession at a Catholic church

Despite the many years Europeans have had contact with The Gambia, there are few Christians. Almost all are found in Banjul or directly south near the Senegalese border. The Akus are Methodists and the Anglican church has some followers. The Roman Catholics are the largest group, comprising mostly Senegalese settled in Banjul. Another group of Catholics are the Jolas, located near the Senegalese border in the western part of the country. In February 1992 they were honored by a visit from Pope John Paul II, who visited Banjul during a trip to several African countries. But few Gambians are attracted to Christianity because it is associated with Europeans who, after enslaving them, colonized them. Islam was introduced by other African groups. It provided a rallying point for resistance to Europeans in The Gambia and Gambians now consider it the true African religion.

Chapter 7

NUTS, NUTS, NUTS

THE ECONOMIC SITUATION

The Gambia is a poor country with few natural resources besides agricultural land. The Gambia has no natural resources of any importance. Nothing remains of the iron deposits. Gambians believe that gold, diamonds, and mercury exist, but nothing of value has ever been found.

The people grow peanuts, rice, millet, sorghum, corn, and palm trees for oil and kernels. They tend livestock and catch fish. Seventy-five percent of the country's income comes from selling agricultural products. Almost all of this is peanuts, although fresh vegetables are also being sold in European markets.

There is very little industry, with the exception of a mill for processing peanuts into peanut oil, one that brews citrus drinks, and another that manufactures beer (Julbrew) for the expatriate European and tourist market. Some agricultural machinery is assembled, and there is a small quantity of woodworking and metalworking. Clothing is fashioned from imported cloth. But almost everything that is not food, including oil, must be bought from other countries. Imports include textiles, machinery, transport equipment, and fuel. Even extra food is often required. The money to purchase these chiefly comes from peanut earnings. These products are bought from France, Great Britain, and several Asian countries.

Over the years The Gambia has grown and exported one crop that does well in its soil and climate: the peanut. This situation is dangerous, because if The Gambia can only sell a portion of its peanut harvest or the price drops, the country has no other important product to replace it.

The Gambia cannot pay for all it buys abroad. Some of this debt is paid through foreign aid. But The Gambia's debt has become large enough to cause international finance and development agencies to require the government to adopt the Economic Recovery Program. This plan aims to promote agricultural development, particularly exports, to earn money to pay off debts. It also proposes to decrease the number of people employed by the government. In the last decade tourism has been developed and has been relatively successful, with nearly one hundred thousand tourists visiting The Gambia's pristine beaches from November to March. Today, tourism ranks second only to peanuts as a source of income for the country. But its value and the number of Gambians employed in tourism is still tiny, when compared with the peanut industry.

PEANUTS

In the sixteenth century the Portuguese brought from their Brazilian colony a vinelike plant that produced peanuts. The Gambians cultivated this plant because it was nourishing and

A mechanical sorter puts peanuts into sacks before they are shipped.

grew well. Corn and manioc, first domesticated by Amerindians, were also brought from across the Atlantic.

Until the early nineteenth century the peanut was just one of several cultivated plants, and the nuts were consumed only by the people who grew them. However, after the British outlawed slavery, they decided that they would encourage farmers to grow many more peanuts, which could be exported to Britain to be made into oil for cooking, machine lubricants, and soap. In 1830 one basket of peanuts was exported from The Gambia; by 1848 the small colony exported more than eight thousand tons (more than seven million kilograms). The colony's administrators received revenues from a tax on the peanuts that left the country.

The peanut is a plant of many uses that adapts well to many areas in the tropics. The nut can be sold whole or crushed. When crushed it produces a valuable, tasteless oil used in cooking, as salad oil, and in the manufacture of margarine, soap, and cooking fat. The solid material left after the nut is crushed is called groundnut cake. It makes a nutritious fodder for animals. These products contain a large amount of protein.

The Gambia is a country of farms and peasant farmers. Outside of Banjul, everyone clears a patch of land to grow peanuts at the beginning of each rainy season. This includes merchants, artisans, marabouts, and musicians. Townspeople can be found tending their fields on the outskirts in the early morning before going to work. The government buys the nuts at the end of the dry season and exports them through an organization called the Produce Marketing Board.

But there is a price to be paid for growing peanuts throughout the country. Basing a country's economy on the lowly peanut confines its people to a weak earner of foreign exchange.

OTHER EFFORTS FOR INCOME

Efforts to find alternative income sources and to increase food crops have not been lacking. Cash crops for export that have been investigated are limes, avocados, papaws (papayas), bananas, cashews, and tobacco. But there are problems. The Gambia has a poor transport system, inefficient marketing, and tough competition from elsewhere in the world. The Gambia does not produce large enough quantities for ocean freighters to bother to stop and pick them up.

The effort to create new food crops has centered on growing rice. The rice plant produces more food per plant than all the other cereal grasses except corn. Rice production has increased

A Gambian farmer and his son plow the family field.

somewhat over the past decades, but not enough to avoid the need to buy rice abroad.

The average Gambian farmer uses traditional farming methods. To increase the farmer's productivity the government made an effort in the 1960s to replace the usual hand hoe with ox plowing. It also taught farmers about fertilizers and insecticides. By the late 1960s the agriculture department was recommending small, one-cylinder tractors to replace the oxen. These small, simple tractors seemed to make sense in a country where normal-size tractors are far too expensive, too large for the small plots of land, and too difficult to repair because parts and mechanics are scarce. However, even these tractors are expensive, and fuel and spare parts must be imported. Researchers are currently working to improve the traditional practices farmers have developed over thousands of years as a way to increase agricultural production.

A woman harvests some of her vegetables.

Traditional agricultural practices also have the advantage of being adjustable to the wide variation from year to year in the climate. In the Sahel the climate is cyclical. From the 1940s to 1970 it was relatively wet. Dry conditions prevailed from the 1970s to 1980. In the 1990s, the area has been wet again.

One additional source of income that has developed successfully is fishing. The fish catch in 1974 was 15,000 tons (13,500 metric tons). In 1981 it was 39,000 tons (35,000 metric tons) and growing. Half of the catch in the 1980s was exported. Unfortunately, fishing fleets from foreign countries have plundered these offshore resources of the Atlantic so that the number of fish that can be caught is limited for the present.

Chapter 8

OTHER ECONOMIC ASPECTS

TRANSPORTATION

For a country's economy to do well it is necessary that the movement of goods and people be as efficient as possible. The Gambia is a small country, so transportation should not be difficult. The Gambia is located near one of the world's important transcontinental air routes and shipping lanes, so connections to the outside world should be excellent. Instead, the opposite is true, in both cases.

Senegambia is a major stopping point along the air routes between Europe and South America, between Western Europe and southern Africa and between North America and Africa. Located halfway along these routes, with the Sahara on one side and the Atlantic on the other, Senegambia is the perfect place for changing planes and refueling. At the beginning of the twentieth century both Dakar and Banjul had small airports. Banjul was picked by Lufthansa, the German airline, as its main airport for this part of the world. But because the British did not develop the airport, Lufthansa eventually left. Today the airport is used for local

A car ferry at Banjul's port

flights and a few regularly scheduled flights to Europe. Dakar's airport, on the other hand, was developed by the French. It is one of the most important outside Europe and North America. Banjul sits in its shadow.

Much the same story can be told about Banjul's port. Senegambia is located at a point in western Africa where the shipping routes between Europe and the Middle East, southern Africa, and Asia pass close by. Dakar has taken advantage of this to develop into a primary port. But Banjul's port is small and inefficient. Despite port expansion projects of the 1970s and 1980s, Banjul's port remains limited. Most large ships cannot dock but must anchor in the river's mouth and send and receive cargo by using small boats. Today Dakar's port is full of oceangoing freighters and tankers, but Banjul is visited by only an occasional ship.

The Gambia is one of the three West African countries that does not have a railroad. The Gambia does not need a railroad because

Repairing a road in Banjul

of its size, but what is serious is that no railroad goes through the country to connect it to other places. Once again this country finds itself quite isolated from its neighbors and the world.

There are, of course, roads. But in general, they are in poor condition. Most are not surfaced and become impassable in the rainy season. The total absence of bridges means that trucks and cars must either stay on one side of the river or suffer a long wait in line to take a ferry across.

Along the Gambia River there is only local trade. The river is difficult to navigate. Sand lying at the bottom is piled into treacherous banks by the currents. Under the British the sandbanks were dredged on a regular basis. But today The Gambia is too poor to buy or rent dredging equipment. In recent decades many ferries and river steamers have sunk after hitting river sandbars. Although these sunken boats are a hazard, they have not been salvaged.

Like much else in The Gambia, the traffic that does use the

river is slow and calm. In winter motor launches carry cash sent upriver by the Banjul trading firms to their peanut-buying agents. In the spring, small freighters sail to Kaur and Kuntaur to load shelled peanuts and return to Banjul. Near Banjul, small yachts take tourists upriver to view the mangrove forests and village life. All year long Serere fishers from Senegal go back and forth in small decorated boats. And all year long the government boat carries the mail and passengers and their loads from one river station to another.

Most river stations consist of a ramshackle old wharf next to a shedlike building. When the government boat reaches the pier, villagers rush down the road that ends at the station. They come to sell chickens, eggs, cakes, papaya, straw mats, and wicker chairs to the passengers. At the same time, others jump off the ship to sell ribbons, balloons, cloth, plastic hairpins, noisemakers, and other trinkets to the villagers. The mail is dropped off. People going down to Banjul or returning from there, get on or off with their belongings. When the ship's whistle gives a piercing hoot, the bargaining between sellers and buyers gets serious. As the boat slowly begins to move, prices come down as villagers and shipboard traders yell and gesture at each other. Just before several feet of water between them threatens to break off negotiations, prices drop considerably. Everyone laughs as mats, chairs, eggs, fish, and bread fly through the air in one direction while coins fly in the other.

TOURISM: WAVE OF THE FUTURE?

The efforts of Gambians to make money other than in peanuts are endless. The government has offered generous tax and

Tourists are entertained on boat excursions (left) and encouraged to participate in local celebrations (right).

customs incentives to attract foreign industry. Not much has come of this, but there is one exception to the bleak economic picture.

In 1976 the Gambians embarked on a long-term project that they hoped would have more success than previous similar attempts. This was to attract foreign tourists. In that year a portion of the Atlantic coastline was declared a Tourist Development Area. Here the roads and the water, electricity, and sewerage systems needed for tourist establishments were constructed with the help of international lenders. A farm was set up to experiment with growing food that tourists would find familiar.

The occupants of the hotels built along the Atlantic beaches are principally Germans, Scandinavians, and British. These northern Europeans wish to escape the cold and the gray, rainy days of winter.

Tourists take safaris to the reserved areas.

The Gambia has some important advantages over competing tourist areas. It is far cheaper than much older centers like Italy and Spain, even though it is farther away. It is closer to Europe than the Caribbean, and unlike Senegal, it is an English-speaking country. (Virtually all Scandinavians speak English.) The Gambia does not have revolutions every few years, civil wars, or terrorists.

In 1988-1989, 120,000 tourists came, staying on the average for a week or two. This was twice the number that visited five years previously. Besides the northern Europeans there have been an increasing number of French visitors who visit Senegal and then drive or fly down to The Gambia. With publication of Haley's *Roots,* a growing number of African-Americans are arriving to make a pilgrimage to Juffure on the river's north bank. The income these diverse visitors provide represents 7.5 percent of The

The Gambians genuinely like having visitors. This crowd of villagers is saying farewell to a group of tourists.

Gambia's wealth. Plans have been made to improve the airport and to increase the number of hotel rooms. The tourist boom has provided needed seasonal employment for at least 5,000 young Gambians.

While the economic impact on the country has been positive, the government is aware that it could be considerably better. Until recently most of what the tourists paid stayed in Europe. They flew on planes owned by Europeans, lived in hotels owned and operated by tourist organizations in Scandinavia, and had their trip organized by a European travel agency. If they were unaccustomed to or disliked the African food, frozen and canned European food had to be imported. While the government obviously did not want to scare the tourists and the tourist agencies away, it felt the situation was unfair. Laws were passed and now hotel and local travel bills must be paid to Gambians.

The young Gambians are
being prepared for the future.

A woman being treated at a clinic

THE FUTURE

Before and immediately after The Gambia became independent everyone believed this tiny sliver of a country was destined to disappear quickly. Instead, the unexpected has happened. Though still struggling economically, its future looks brighter than it has for some time. Its relatively calm and democratic politics and its efforts to protect its own and the world's wildlife have given it international respect. And its people, joyful and at peace with life and each other, are a model that many can look up to.

To the surprise of everybody, The Gambia has been a success since independence. It still exists. It remains one of the few democracies of Africa, despite the short but bloody revolution in 1981. It has overcome various economic crises due to changes of climate and world markets. And it has created a national spirit among the many different groups that live in the country. Although still poor and still small, The Gambia reaches the end of the twentieth century in far better condition than it was a hundred years earlier.

Playing an old game called wouré

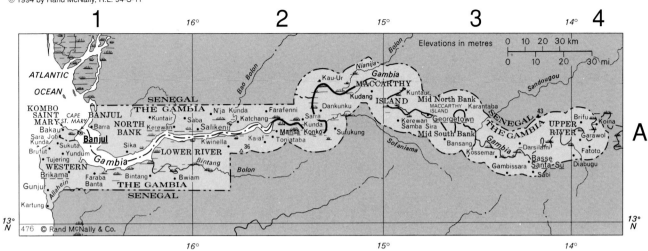

MAP KEY

Allahein (river)	A1	Kerewan	A1
Atlantic Ocean	A1	Kerewan Samba Sira	A3
Bakau	A1	Koina	A4
Banjul	A1	Kombo Saint Mary (district)	A1
Banjul (district)	A1	Kossemar	A3
Bansang	A3	Kudang	A2
Barra	A1	Kuntair	A1
Basse Santa Su	A3	Kuntaur	A3
Bintang	A1	Kwinella	A2
Bintang (river)	A1, A2	Lower River (district)	A1, A2
Brifu	A4	MacCarthy Island	A3
Brikama	A1	MacCarthy Island (district)	A2, A3
Brufut	A1	Mansa Konko	A2
Bwiam	A1	Mid North Bank	A3
Cape St. Mary	A1	Mid South Bank	A3
Dankunku	A2	Nianija (river)	A2, A3
Darsilami	A3	N'ja Kunda	A2
Diabugu	A4	North Bank (district)	A1, A2
Faraba Banta	A1	Saba	A1
Fatoto	A4	Sabi	A3
Farafenni	A2	Salikeni	A2
Gambia (river)	A1, A2, A3, A4	Sara Kunda	A1
Gambissara	A3	Sarra Kunda	A2
Garawol	A4	Sika	A1
Georgetown	A3	Sofaniama (river)	A2, A3
Gunju	A1	Sukuta	A1
Job	A1	Sutukung	A2
Kaiaf	A2	Toniataba	A2
Karantaba	A3	Tujering	A1
Kartung	A1	Upper River (district)	A3, A4
Katchang	A2	Western (district)	A1, A2
Kau-Ur	A2	Yundum	A1

113

MINI-FACTS AT A GLANCE

GENERAL INFORMATION

Official Name: Republic of The Gambia

Capital: Banjul

Government: The Gambia is a multiparty republic with one legislative house. The executive branch consists of a president, vice-president, and a cabinet. The president is elected every 5 years and is the head of state and government. The 50-member House of Representatives includes 5 indirectly elected tribal chiefs, 4 presidential nominees, and 6 appointees. The country's highest judicial body is the Supreme Court. The Gambia is one of Africa's long-standing democratic countries.

For administrative purpose the country is divided into 6 territorial divisions (council areas) and one city, Banjul. Banjul is run by an elected town council.

Religion: Although the Gambian constitution does not support an official religion, more than 90 percent of the population follows Islam. The remainder of the populace practices either Christianity (chiefly Methodism and Anglicanism, which is concentrated in the Banjul area) or traditional religions. Traditional African religious practices for medicinal and spiritual healing are quite important to Gambians regardless of religious beliefs.

Ethnic Composition: The major ethnic groups of The Gambia, in descending order of importance, are: Mandinka (40 percent), Fulani (19 percent), Wolof (15 percent), Jola (10 percent), and Serrahuli (8 percent). The dominant Mandinka are rural farmers and traders and the country's principal rice growers. The Fulani are concentrated in the central and eastern part of the country and raise cattle for a living; they follow transhumant herding, moving their cattle from the plateau to the lowlands during the dry season. Wolof are concentrated in Banjul and near the Senegalese borders. They are engaged in trade, civil service, and farming. The Jola live in the western part of the country south of the Gambia River; they also are farmers. Most of the country's commerce is controlled by Serrahuli and Lebanese and Syrian traders, while a small group of Europeans reside in The Gambia as advisers, businessmen, and diplomats.

Language: English is the official language, but its use outside the capital is limited. Some 21 distinct languages are spoken in The Gambia, of which Wolof and Mandinka are the most widely used.

National Flag: Adopted in 1965, the flag is a tricolor of red, blue, and green horizontal stripes separated by two narrow white stripes. The blue stripe running through the center of the flag represents the Gambia River. The green stands for agricultural resources, red stands for the sun, and white symbolizes unity and peace.

National Emblem: Two heraldic lions hold a blue shield displaying a hoe and ax. At the crest is a blue knight's helmet, a green oil palm, and peanuts sprouting from a mound. On the scroll below is the national motto: "Progress, Peace, Prosperity."

National Anthem: "For Gambia Our Homeland"

National Calendar: Gregorian, but the lunar Muslim calendar regulates daily life for most of the country's inhabitants.

Money: One *dalasi* (D) of 100 *butut* is the official currency. In 1993 one dalasi was worth $0.09 in United States currency.

Membership in International Organizations: African Development Bank (AfDB); Inter-American Development Bank (IDB); International Monetary Fund (IMF); International Rice Council (IRC); Nonaligned Movement (NAM); Organization of African Unity (OAU); United Nations (UN)

Weights and Measures: Both the Imperial and metric system are used.

Population: 932,000, (1993 estimates); density 214 persons per sq. mi. (83 persons per sq km); 77 percent rural, 23 percent urban

Cities:

Greater Banjul	145,692 (1983 census)
Serekunda	102,600 (1986 estimate)
Brikama	24,300 (1986 estimate)
Bakau	23,600 (1986 estimate)
Farafenni	10,168 (1983 census)
Sukuta	7,227 (1983 census)
Gunjar	7,115 (1983 census)

GEOGRAPHY

Border: The Gambia is almost surrounded by Senegal except in the west where the country reaches to the Atlantic Ocean. The land boundary with Senegal is 470 mi. (756 km) long.

Land: The Gambia is a low and flat country stretched along the banks of the Gambia River. The country is little more than a river basin located within Senegal. The three major physical regions include: the coast, the flat lowlands along the river, and the slightly higher and drier uplands. The coastal area is comprised of sandy beaches, which favors the country's attraction for tourism. Floodplains exist on either side of the Gambia River with mangrove swamps dominating the brackish water area from the coast to the central river region. The *banto faros*, areas that have firm ground in the dry season but become rice-growing swamps during the rains, are located behind mangrove swamps. The sandstone uplands favored for peanut cultivation are above river flooding and cover the rest of the country. The majority of the population lives along the boundary of the lowland and upland region where they can farm two distinct ecological zones.

Highest Point: 239 ft. (72 m)

Lowest Point: Sea level

Rivers: The Gambia River is one of West Africa's key physical features. A major artery to the interior, it reaches 1,100 mi. (1,770 km) inland. At the estuary the river broadens from 4 to 5 mi. (6 to 8 km) wide. The river is navigable to about 150 mi. (240 km) upstream. The ocean floods the river channels of the estuary causing saltwater to flow 56 mi. (90 km) upriver. Between 56 mi. and 155 mi. (250 km) the river is mixed salt and freshwater; above that point freshwater is found in the river.

Forests: Some 16 percent of the country's territory is covered by forests. Grassland or savanna vegetation dominates, consisting of tall grass and scattered trees. Mangroves grow along the lower riverbanks and near the mouth of the Gambia River. The uplands are covered with grasses and crops during the rainy season, but the trees and bushes shrivel up and turn yellow in the dry season. During the rains the countryside abounds with many flowers like yellow cassias and scarlet combretum and tropical shrubs such as bougainvillea, oleander, and numerous varieties of hibiscus.

The tall and elegant kapok or silk cotton tree dominates village life, providing fluffy white flowers that are used to stuff mattresses. Palm trees abound in low-lying swamps and give many useful products like fruit, cooking oil, and wine. The baobab tree, also found close to villages, provides sweet-smelling flowers, edible fruit, and medicinal leaves; its bark is made into paper, rope, and cloth, and its seeds are used to make fertilizer and soap. Mangrove wood is used for firewood, home building, and carving traditional objects.

Wildlife: The few large animals found in The Gambia are located in the river or along the river's banks. They include crocodiles, hippopotamuses, West African manatees, eland, waterbucks, boars, monitor lizards, pythons, an occasional leopard, and the large wading bird, the ibis. Found away from the river and its creeks are warthogs, baboons, monkeys, pangolins, aardvarks, and dwarf antelopes. Wildlife is protected and preserved in several nature reserves and the Baboon Island National Park.

The Gambia is a significant country for bird watching. During the winter months more than four hundred species of migratory birds stopover luring European bird-watchers, who represent more than 10 percent of the country's tourists. Favored birds for viewing include hawks, eagles, buzzards, francolins, crows, pintailed weavers, wydah birds, and ospreys.

Climate: The climate is subtropical with a distinct wet and hot season lasting from June to October and a dry and hot season from November to May. Temperatures in the interior average nearly 100° F. (37.7° C) annually but grow hotter in the dry season and more muggy during the rains. Along the coast temperatures may drop to 60° F. (15.5° C) in the night during the cooler months of December and January. The dry season frequently brings *harmattan* winds, which carry sand that blows from the Sahara; these dust blizzards can reduce visibility to just a few feet. Annual rainfall ranges from 36 in. (92 cm) in the interior to 57 in. (145 cm) along the coast, but varies by as much as 25 percent from year to year. As the rainy season begins, the river and its tributaries flood.

Greatest Distance: North to south, 30 mi. (48 km)
East to west, 292 mi. (470 km)

Area: 4,361 sq. mi. (11,295 sq km).

ECONOMY AND INDUSTRY

Agriculture: About one-sixth of the country is considered arable. Land is owned by the village and divided among the families who usually have areas along the floodplains and on the uplands for planting rice and peanuts, respectively. Cultivation of rice is done almost exclusively by women. Cotton, corn, manioc, millet, and sorghum also are grown on the uplands, while bananas and vegetables are additionally planted on the flat swampy lands. Three-fourths of the country's income comes from selling agricultural products, chiefly peanuts, in the international market.

The Gambia River provides rural people with most of their protein needs. Fishers catch shrimp, oysters, and crabs in the mangrove swamp area. From the ocean are caught game fish like marlin, barracuda, wrasse, flying fish, yellowtail, snapper, catfish, rock hind mullet, sea bream, dorado, sailfish, bonito, swordfish, shark, sunfish, and mackerel tuna. Much of the country's specialized coastal fishing is concentrated south of Banjul near the Senegalese border at Gunjar. Traditional fishers are now involved in commercial fishing with help from the government; their fishing boats are fitted with motors, smoking ovens, and freezers.

Mining: The Gambia has very few commercially important minerals. There are a few iron ore deposits; sand and gravel areas for extraction locally; and small reserves of zirconium and kaolin. Offshore drilling is underway for potential oil reserves.

Manufacturing: There is very little industry in The Gambia. Small manufacturing plants produce peanut and palm kernel oil, citrus beverages, textiles, and leather works. Peanut oil is used in cooking, as salad oil, and in the manufacturing of margarine, soap, and cooking fat. The solid material remaining from crushing the peanut for oil provides a nutritious fodder for animals. Some agricultural machinery is assembled in the country and there is a small quantity of woodworking and metalworking. Electricity is generated entirely from imported fuels.

Tourism: The government has been promoting tourism as an additional source of income besides peanut farming and commercial fisheries. A portion of the Atlantic coastline south of Banjul forms the tourist development area with its infrastructure of roads, running water, electricity, and sewage systems. Most of the tourists visiting The Gambia are German, Scandinavian, French, and British.

Transportation: The Gambia is one of the few countries in Africa with no railroads. Travel is by boat and road. To go north of the river to Barra, the Juffure of Alex Haley, and into Senegal requires crossing the broad estuary by ferry. Ferries also operate across the river at Farafenni and Georgetown. Banjul is connected to the mainland by a bridge across the swamp. There are about 1,500 mi. (2,400 km) of roads, of which about one-third are paved. The Trans-Gambian Highway connecting northern and southern Senegal goes through central Gambia at Farafenni. The north bank road (unpaved) and the south bank road connect many of the villages on both sides of the river, which also are accessible to the river by dirt trails that run at right angles from the village to river landings. The Gambia River is used by motor launches, small freighters, and government mail boats. The river is sometimes difficult to use because of underlying sandbars. Banjul is a major seaport along the West African coast. The international airport is at Yundum, 16 mi. (26 km) from Banjul.

Communication: The Gambia has one daily newspaper with a circulation of about 1,000. In the early 1990s there was one radio receiver per 5 persons and just one telephone per 80 persons. Telephone service remains concentrated in the capital area. The country does not have television service at present. Radio Gambia broadcasts in English and other African languages.

Trade: Chief imports are food (especially rice and wheat flour), machinery and transport equipment, textiles, petroleum, chemicals, and manufactured goods. Major import sources are Great Britain, China, France, Germany, Hong Kong, Belgium, and Luxembourg. Chief export items are peanuts, fish, and winter vegetables. Major export destinations are Belgium, Luxembourg, New Zealand, Guinea, Great Britain, France, and Switzerland.

EVERYDAY LIFE

Health: The major health problems are malaria, gastroenteritis, dysentery, pneumonia, measles, bronchitis, and whooping cough. The Gambia has one of the highest death rates in the world. Life expectancy at 44 years for males and 47 years for females is low, even for Western Africa. The infant mortality rate at 132 per 1,000 live births is very high. The government, in conjunction with foreign organizations, has improved the availability of immunization programs in rural Gambia but access to medical care is poor and contributes to low life expectancy. Folk medicine dominates medical care in villages.

Education: Primary education is free but not compulsory, but there is a shortage of schoolteachers in rural Gambia. School begins at 8 years of age and lasts for 6 years. Secondary high school is for 5 years and secondary technical school is for 4 years. Children in rural areas may have no school nearby and often have to tend cattle, help in farming, or take care of the younger siblings. As a result, many school age children in rural areas do not attend school. There is no university in the country, but a 2-year college at Banjul offers courses in teacher training, agriculture, and health. Every year a dozen or so Gambian students get full scholarship to attend universities abroad. In the early 1990s the literacy rate was about 27 percent.

Holidays:
> January 1, New Year's Day
> February 18, Independence Day, National Day
> April 24, Republic Day
> August 15, the Queen's Birthday

Islamic holidays are Id al-Fitr, Id al-Adha, and Milad an-Nabi. Christian festivals include Christmas, Good Friday, and Easter Monday.

Culture: Gambian people express themselves through wood carving, batik cloth painting, weaving, and gold and silver jewelry making. Tradition and history are very much a part of village life with everyone learning the myths, lore, history, and knowledge required to function as a member of a Gambian community. Islam is a way of daily life for rural Gambians; almost all villages have a simple mosque for worshiping. The *imam* is the chief religious leader who teaches young people religious ideals. The Gambia's chief cultural institutions include the National Library and the National Museum, both in Banjul.

Society: Extended families from the same clan live in large compounds and form a social security network by helping each other with work and sometimes financially. When a woman marries, she moves to her husband's compound. The *bantaba*, a perched platform of logs under the village's main shade tree, is the village meeting place. The *griot* is the local historian and storyteller. The village chief works for better relations between the village and the government and the government pays him a small salary and pension. The chief and the oldest males form a council that keeps order and justice within the village.

Rural women are the chief farmers of rice, the food staple. In addition to hard work in the swamps, they haul water from the well, pound grain, cook, do housework, and take care of the children. They seldom are educated and they have very few opportunities to earn cash. Despite their work burdens, women help one another. They share work by belonging to collective groups called kafos, which function as women's social security networks. If a woman is sick, other kafo members will do her work.

Dress: Due to the hot climate, loose-fitting clothes are preferred by both men and women. Men wear *caftans* or *warambas*, long gowns with elongated armholes, over baggy trousers. Women also wear caftans, but more frequently a blouse and a *faneau*, a piece of cloth wrapped around the body and tucked into the waist to form a skirt. A brightly colored cloth is usually wrapped around a woman's head as a turban, which adds a nice accent to the bright-colored garb. Inexpensive rubber sandals are worn by almost everyone. Western-style clothing is popular in cities.

Housing: Typical city buildings are two stories high with shops on street level and living quarters above. Outside walls are usually painted in pastels: pink, blue, green, or cream. The colonial buildings left from the British era have balconies, shutters, and dormer windows. Houses are raised on pillars to improve air circulation and minimize flooding. In poorer urban areas, several one-room wood or tin-roof houses are clustered around dirt courtyards. A village is formed by groups of compounds with houses in concentric circles. Village huts have mud walls and tin or thatch roofs. As most life takes place outside, they have few windows to minimize the entry of mosquitoes. Some homes have verandas in front. Sheep, goats, and chickens are kept in the adjoining courtyard and cattle are grazed in nearby fields.

Food: The Gambian diet consists chiefly of grains (rice, corn, millet, or sorghum) that are consumed at every meal. A porridge of rice or millet is eaten for breakfast while other meals contain wonderful sauces often made from peanuts. Rice is eaten with sauces prepared from dried fish, pounded raw peanuts, vegetables, or palm oil. Favorite cooked dishes are *benachin*, a rice-based fish stew made with vegetables, and *domada*, a spicy peanut sauce with meat and vegetables. While warthogs are found throughout rural Gambia, most of its residents do not eat them as pork is forbidden by Islam (as is alcohol).

Recreation: Drums are the most important musical instrument used by Gambians. Drums are traditionally considered sacred and used for special occasions. Beating the drum is accompanied by dancing or hand clapping or both. Another traditional instrument is the *cora*, a large string instrument fashioned from a gourd that produces a harplike sound. Flutes and bowlike fiddles also are played. Another favorite instrument is the *balafon*, a type of xylophone or marimba, made from gourds of different sizes. African pop and Reggae music of the West Indies are popular among young adults.

Social Welfare: There are no public social welfare programs in the country. Communities and clans generally take care of their old and sick relatives. *Kafo* groups are a Gambian woman's insurance fund since the female members work together and support each other in times of personal or financial crisis.

IMPORTANT DATES

A.D. 800-1200–Senegambian Stone Circles are constructed

1432–Portuguese expeditions to the south of Cape Bojador start

1444–Portuguese reach the mouth of the Senegal River

1445–Portuguese arrive at the Gambia River estuary

1588–Portuguese sell exclusive trade rights on the Gambia River to English merchants

1618–James I of England grants a charter to a British company for trade with The Gambia and the Gold Coast (now Ghana)

1651–Courland traders arrive to look for slaves to send to the Caribbean colony of Tobago

1661–English traders oust the Courlanders and take over the slave trade

1681–The French Senegal Company builds a trading post at Albreda opposite James Island

1783–The Treaty of Versailles gives possession of The Gambia to Great Britain

1807–Great Britain abolishes the Atlantic slave trade

1816–Lord Bathurst orders construction of a new fort at Saint Mary's island site; the fort later becomes the city of Banjul

1819–Banjul has a population of seven hundred

1823–The first group of Wesleyan Methodist missionaries arrives

1825–Banjul has a population of fourteen hundred

1830–Peanut exports begin

1843–Banjul becomes a separate British colony

1848–Peanut exports reach more than 8,000 tons (more than 7,000,000 kilograms)

1857–French cede Albreda to the British

1859–Yellow fever epidemic

1866–The Gambia and Sierra Leone are united under a single administration

1888–The Gambia becomes a British protectorate; the Colony of The Gambia is separated from Sierra Leone and is given its own governor

1889–Anglo-French Convention defines the boundary of The Gambia; The Gambia becomes a British colony

1893–British establish "indirect rule" in The Gambia protectorate

1901–The Gambia receives its own executive and legislative councils

1906–An ordinance abolishes indigenous slavery in The Gambia

1957–Ghana becomes an independent country

1959–People' Progressive Party (PPP) is formed

1960–Preparation for independence following Nigeria this year; general elections are held in The Gambia

1961–Sierra Leone becomes an independent country

1962–The constitution gives full self-rule to Gambians; Dauda Kairaba Jawara becomes prime minister

1965–The Gambia becomes an independent country within the British Commonwealth; proposal to become a republic is defeated in a referendum

1967–The Gambia signs a defense treaty with Senegal

1970–In the second referendum voters approve The Gambia leaving the Commonwealth; The Gambia becomes a republic; the present constitution takes effect

1971–The dalasi is introduced as the Gambian national currency

1972–President Jawara is reelected

1973–The capital city of Bathurst is officially renamed Banjul

1976–Alex Haley publishes *Roots: The Saga of an American Family*; The Gambian government launches a long-term project to promote tourism

1977–President Jawara signs the Banjul Declaration to protect The Gambia's wildlife

1980–Sir Jawara is awarded a medal by the Food and Agriculture Organization (FAO) of the United Nations for his efforts to lessen the destructive impacts of droughts; the Organization of African Unity's Human Rights Summit meeting takes place in The Gambia

1981–Sir Jawara goes to London to attend the wedding of Prince Charles and Princess Diana, revolutionary forces seize power in Banjul in his absence, a state of emergency is declared and many people killed; democracy is restored with Senegalese troops after a three-day fight; the Confederation of the Senegambia is formed

1987–Sir Jawara is reelected president

1988-89–Tourism reaches 120,000

1989–The Senegambian Confederation is officially dissolved

1990–The government undertakes a long-term restructuring of the education system; The Gambia sends armed troops to Liberia to enforce a cease-fire in Liberia's civil war

1991–The Gambia and Senegal sign a bilateral agreement of friendship and cooperation

1992–Pope John Paul II visits Banjul; Sir Jawara is reelected as president for the sixth time; a postage stamp is issued in memory of the Scottish explorer Mungo Park; in general elections Sir Jawara is reelected and the People's Progressive party wins 25 seats

1993–The World Conference on Human Rights takes place in The Gambia

IMPORTANT PEOPLE

Alex Palmer Haley (1921-93), African-American writer who traced his family's origins to the north bank of the Gambia River. His book, *Roots: The Saga of an American Family* (1976), won a special Pulitzer prize in 1976

Alhaji Sir Dauda Kairaba Jawara (1924-   ), veterinarian, the country's first prime minister (1962 to 1970) and first president (since 1970), most recently elected in 1992

Mungo Park (1771-1806), Scottish explorer; he led an expedition through The Gambia in search of the source of the Niger River in 1795 for Great Britain's African Association. His journey was published as *Travels in the Interior of Africa* (1799).

Compiled by Chandrika Kaul

INDEX

Page numbers that appear in boldface type indicate illustrations

125

About the Author

Robert Zimmermann was born in Lima, Peru, and has lived in Thailand, Britain, Spain, and Portugal as well as the United States. He received a B.A. (Cum Laude) from Clark University and an M.A. from George Washington University, both in geography. For more than fifteen years he lived in Chicago where he taught world geography and twentieth-century world history in a private high school. Currently he is teaching high school in New York City. In 1982-83, Mr. Zimmermann spent a year in Nassau as a Lecturer in Geography and Social Studies at the College of the Bahamas. He has published a map of Chicago for tourists and a journal article on a course he has taught about Russia and Austria. Recently he was given the Award for Excellence in Teaching Geography by the Geographical Society of Chicago. Mr. Zimmermann is the author of *Sri Lanka*, also in the Enchantment of the World series.